**Boğaç Aybey**

# About "The Last Song" by Nickolas Sparks. Journal, Essay and Vocabulary

GRIN Verlag

**Bibliografische Information der Deutschen Nationalbibliothek:**

Die Deutsche Bibliothek verzeichnet diese Publikation in der Deutschen Nationalbibliografie; detaillierte bibliografische Daten sind im Internet über http://dnb.d-nb.de/ abrufbar.



**Imprint:**


Druck und Bindung: Books on Demand GmbH, Norderstedt Germany
ISBN: 978-3-656-75753-5

**This book at GRIN:**

http://www.grin.com/en/e-book/281075/about-the-last-song-by-nickolas-sparks-journal-essay-and-vocabulary

## THE LAST SONG

The Last Song is written by #1 New York Times Bestselling author Nicholas Sparks and released on [1]September 8, 2009 by Grand Central Publishing . Also it was the number one on the weekly bestseller chart of [2]New York Times Best Sellers List on September 18, 2009 ,and many reviews were written about The Last Song. Besides them, its new movie has been started to play on the cinemas in the U.S.A. since [3]March 31, 2010,so this book is so popular and remarkable, because the characters' behaviours and qualities are created uniquely, the book really impacts on our lives ,and some religious informations and sacred books are related with the characters' situations and the events in the book.

First of all, the writer creates the characters and gives them some behaviours uniquely. Firstly , the change in Ronnie from a stubborn girl to a mature young lady makes the book more remarkable and special. For example, the novel states that "It was the first time since she'd been here that she'd spoken to him without a hint of anger or frustration. " (pg.104)"In profile, he could see both the young woman she was becoming and the little girl he remembered."(pg. 105) From these quotes we learn that at the beginning she seems like a stubborn, grouchy and bad tempered girl, and her decisions, behaviours and relationship with her dad, brother, and Blaze seems untrue. Then she joins to a bad crowd which includes the antagonist Marcus ,but she changes gradually after she falls in love with Will, so she becomes a lovely, live, kind, grateful and honest girl instead of a girl who does the opposite of what her parents say to her or what she must do ,and it leads the reader to think about their relationships. Another character is definitely Jonah and, the writer creates Jonah as an amazingly funny, sarcastic, enthusiastic and playful character and mostly optimistic. For instance, "Oh," Jonah said, thinking. "Tell him you didn't see me." Jonah thought about it. "Five bucks." "What?" "Gimme five bucks and I'll forget you were here." "Are you serious?" "You don't have much time," he said. "Now it's ten bucks." (...) "You missed your chance. But your secret will be safe with me." (pg.32) "Hey, is this your house?" "That's it." "This place is awesome!" (pg.15). Also , I love the way he tricks his sister, and reacts to their situations and to Ronnie. Furthermore, from this quote, the reader see that he is too optimistic, so he finds his father's old and ruined house funny and awesome even though the house is nearly old, small, weak, and some of its objects are missing, so he can find a better way to enjoy, and be cheerful in a miserable, horrible, and uncomfortable house. He can still keep his satisfaction alive with thinking of at the sight of the house. Also he is too enthusiastic, and wants to go to the beach with a great eagerness, and zealous movements. As we see that the characters have got some special and even funny qualities combined with a great harmony of the writer's creativity and the situations of the characters.

Another reason why this book is remarkable is that the writer really impacts on our lives. First of all, this novel teaches us that there are significant moments that we mustn't miss them and mustn't regret what we miss. One example of this is "I was so mean to him. I quit the piano! I blamed him for everything, and I didn't say more than a few words to him for three years! Three years! And I can't get those years back. But maybe if I hadn't been so angry, he might not have gotten sick. Maybe I caused that extra... stress that did all this. Maybe it was me!"(pg. 321) This proves that Ronnie regrets that she should spend more time together with her father before he died, because at the beginning she treats her father cruelly and always does the opposite of what he says, so she always goes out,and spends much time with Blaze at the first time that she comes to the beach house ,and after she falls in love with Will, they spend a lot of time together as lovers. Next, there are moments that make me feel full of love and hope such as Will-Ronnie's young love. For instance, the author tells us that "Will was going to go to school here. In New York. With her. And with that, she slipped her arms around him, feeling his body fit perfectly against her own, knowing that nothing could ever be better than this moment, right now.(...) When he met her eyes, she saw the young man she'd loved last summer and the young man she still loved now. "I never stopped loving you, Ronnie. And I never stopped thinking about you. Even if summers do come to an end." She smiled, knowing he was telling the truth. "I love you, too, Will Blakelee," she whispered, leaning in to kiss him again. (pg. 390) It is clear that when Will says that he will stay in New York, I feel the happiness deeply, and am glad that they can see each other ,and their relationship will stay permanently and passionately, so their love will not be a summer love. In conclusion, it is a book which includes a young love, hopes and important moments in our lives, so reality and creativity in this book makes the effect on our lives.

Finally, some religious informations and sacred books are related with the characters' situations and the events in the book appropriately. Firstly, in this novel there are things about presence of God, praying and hope. The novel states that "(...)Never forget that God is your friend. (...)He longs to hear what's been happening in your life. Good or bad, whether it's been full of sorrow or anger, and even when you're questioning why terrible things have to happen. So I talk with him." (pg.165) Pastor Harris laid a reassuring hand on his shoulder. "You have me."(...)"We talk in the same way that you and I do." "Does He answer?" Steve was skeptical. "Always." "You hear Him?" "Yes," (...)"but not with my ears." He put a hand to his chest. "This is where I hear the answers. This is where I feel His presence." (pg.166)From these quotes we learn that the presence of God,praying and hope is developed by Pastor Harris who is an intimate friend of Steve and his piano teacher. Pastor Harris enjoys talking with him about God's presence, Steve's questions and hearing God. Secondly, it is used one part of the Bible to describe the change in Ronnie at the end of the book. On pg. 349 we see that the part (Galatians 5:22) of the Bible in this novel "But when the Holy Spirit controls our lives, he will produce this kind of fruit in us: love, joy, peace, patience, kindness, goodness, faithfulness, gentleness, and self-control." explains the changes in Ronnie the best and fits with Ronnie's situation. Also she finds her first love Will. In addition, she joyfully plays piano for her father ,who suffers from stomach cancer ,and finds the peace in playing piano again since she didn't want to play piano. Besides them, she looks after her fragile father in the hospital with a great patience in her decent heart,and starts to begin behaving in a generous way towards people around her especially her mother and father, so she obeys what they say and want her to do even though at the beginning she does the opposite of what they want like a typical teenager. Furthermore Ronnie devotes herself to her family ,and learns the goodness in people's heart and even in her heart. As a conclusion, connection between some religious books and situations make the book creative and reliable ,and the connection between Ronnie and one part of the Bible really makes the end magnificent and it stays easily in our thoughts as readers.

As a final word, the characters' behaviours, situations and creations are unique, and the book really has an effect on our lives ,and using religious connections make the book more remarkable. Also if someone need a book about love, second chances, hope, forgiveness, being a family, young and even first love, he/she should buy it ,and be a part of its great place, atmosphere, characters and the unsteady and haunting events. This kind of books always make me think and connect my life with the life in this book,and I learn some lessons from them.

[1] [3] http://en.wikipedia.org/wiki/The_Last_Song_%28novel%29

[2]http://www.nytimes.com/2009/09/27/books/bestseller/besthardfiction.html

Boğaç Aybey

## Reader's Response Journal:

**The Last Song** **24.01.10**

**Prologue:**

Quote from this chapter:

**Ronnie: "I was wrong, Mom. And I don't know what to do now. " pg. 2**

Ronnie says to her mother, who comes to her room, when Ronnie looks at her stack of framed photographs from the small beach house where Ronnie stayed last summer. It shows that Ronnie regrets things that she did last summer around the beach house, and doesn't know how she can face with them. Also she is disappointed, and needs help. For example in the book it says "She was eighteen years old and remembering the summer she'd been betrayed, the summer she'd been arrested, the summer she'd fallen in love."

Foreshadowing:

***On the bedstand beside her lay a stack of framed photographs from the alcove of the small beach house,(...) Ronnie continued to stare at the pile of photos, seeing nothing at all. "I was wrong, Mom. And I don't know what to do know."***
***"You mean about your dad?"***
***"About everything." pg.2***

***(...) For an instant, Ronnie felt a crush of memories overwhelm her: the fire and subsequent rebuilding of the church, the stained-glass window, the song she'd finally finished. She thought about Blaze and Scott and Marcus. She thought about Will. She was eighteen years old and remembering the summer she'd been betrayed, the summer she'd been arrested, the summer she'd fallen in love. It hadn't been so long ago, yet sometimes she felt that she'd been an altogether different person back then. pg.2***

I predict that the author will begin to tell Ronnie's last summer with her father in his small beach house. in the next chapter. According to these passages and quotes, she will do wrong and unacceptable things such as to be arrested. Also she will fall in love, and be disappointed in her boyfriend or her best friend. She will have problems with her dad in the beach house, and cannot struggle with them. And the framed photographs from the alcove of the small beach house make her memories of last summer alive. Finally it seems to me that her behaviours, actions, approaches, thoughts, and feelings will change gradually in the next chapters.

**The Last Song** **24.01.10**

**Chapter 1:**

**My Feelings about Characters:**

**Ronnie:** In this chapter, she seems like a usual stubborn teenager, and doesn't want her mother to control her. Also they often argue with each other in the car, and in the beginning she is too grouchy, so it makes their situation worse. I noticed that she doesn't like her father, and she usually accuses him, because he leaves them. Also she is reluctant to spend her summer with her father in his beach house. On the other hand, in her depth she is longing for good old times that are before her parents' divorce, and she expresses her feeling in a sarcastic way.

**Ronnie's mother:** In my opinion she is a peacemaker between her ex-husband, and Ronnie, so she wants her to like him, and takes Jonah and Ronnie to his beach house. Also she loves her daughter, and wants to reassure her by putting Mozart's Sonata No.16 in C Major, which was one of the pieces Ronnie had performed at Carnegie Hall four years ago, while Ronnie was sleeping, but Ronnie wants her to close it. However Ronnie's mother seems as an authoritative figure from Ronnie's point of view, because her mother always has the last word.

**Jonah (Ronnie's brother):** In this chapter, he speaks rarely, but I can say that he is an enthusiastic boy, and definitely loves his father more than Ronnie, so he wants to go to the beach house.

## If I Were ...

***(...) "Ronnie hated the piano and swore she'd never play again, a decision even some of her oldest friends thought was strange, since it had been a major part of her life for as long as she'd known them."(...) pg. 9***

***(...) "She was good, too. Very good, actually, and because of her father's connection to Juilliard, the administration and teachers there were well aware of her ability. (...) A couple of articles in classical music magazines followed, and a moderately long piece in The New York Times that focused on the father-daughter connection came next, all of which eventually led to a coveted appearance in the Young Performers series at Carnegie Hall four years ago. That, she supposed, was the highlight of her career. And it was a highlight; she wasn't naive about what she'd accomplished. She knew how rare an opportunity like that was, but lately she'd found herself wondering whether the sacrifices had been worth it. No one besides her parents probably even remembered the performance, after all. Or even cared. Ronnie had learned that unless you had a popular video on YouTube or could perform shows in front of thousands, musical ability meant nothing."(...)*** **pg.9-10**

If I were Ronnie, I wouldn't stop playing piano, because she is a gifted pianist, and can have a remarkable piano career, so her father is a good and talented pianist, and has got a lot of connections. Also playing piano had been a major part of her life, and I think that it was one think which they shared with her father.

**The Last Song 25.01.10**

**Chapter 2:**

### My Feelings about Characters:

**Steve (Ronnie's father):** His life isn't so untroubled, and peaceful, so he has got problems ever since. For example, "Five years ago, he'd quit his position at Juilliard, and a year after that, he'd decided to try his luck as a concert pianist. Three years ago, he and Kim decided to divorce; less than twelve months later, the tour dates began drying up, until they finally ended completely." is written in this chapter. Also it seems to me that he is excited about his children's arrival, and wants to spend his entire summer with them, so he loves them too much. I noticed that he wants to defend his daughter, Ronnie, even though she doesn't like him.

**Quotes from this chapter:**

***"Hey, is this your house?"***
***"That's it."***
***"This place is awesome!"***
***Steve wondered if Jonah was serious. The house was anything but awesome. The bungalow was easily the oldest property on Wrightsville Beach and sandwiched between two massive homes that had gone up within the last ten years, making it seem even more diminutive. The paint was peeling, the roof was missing numerous shingles, and the porch was rotting; it wouldn't surprise him if the next decent storm blew it over, which would no doubt please the neighbours. Since he'd moved in, neither family had ever spoken to him.***
***"You think so?" he said.***
***"Hello? It's right on the beach. What else could you want?" pg.15***

Jonah says to Steve, when Ronnie, Jonah, and their mother comes to Steve's house, and Jonah rushes toward Steve, and hugs his father intensely. Then they talk about their car travel, and his house. It shows that Jonah is too optimistic even though the house is nearly old, small, weak, and some of its objects are missing, so he can find a better way to enjoy, and be cheerful in a miserable, horrible, and uncomfortable house. He can still keep his satisfaction alive with thinking of at the sight of the house. Also he is too enthusiastic, and wants to go to the beach with a great eagerness, and zealous movements.

**Similar Quotes from Jonah:**
***1) "Are you kidding? This is going to be great!" pg. 8***
***2) "It's the beach," Jonah volunteered. "It's always crowded at the beach." pg. 9***
***3) "Can we go? After we all have dinner together?" pg. 10***
***"I don't know." She sighed. "And I don't think she does, either. She's in this dark, moody phase. She ignores her curfew, and half the time I can't get more than a 'Whatever' when I try to talk to her. I try to write it off as typical teenage stuff, because I remember what it was like... but..." She shook her head. "You saw the way she was dressed, right? And her hair and that god-awful mascara?" pg. 18***

Ronnie's mother says to Steve, when she goes out of the car, and comes near Steve. Then they start to talk about the children's educations, behaviours, manners, problems, and appearances. I think that Ronnie wants to hide her anger for her parents' divorce, and behaves in an insensitive way with not answering or only briefly answering her mother. Also I feel that she thinks that when she dresses like that, she can forget dreadful events that she lives. It seems to me that she wants to act like a teenager, but after her parents' divorce she feels alone, and thinks that everyone in her family goes to their own way, so she can't find a person who understands her feelings, and emotions.

**<u>The Last Song                                                                                    25.01.10</u>**

**Chapter 3:**

Summary of this chapter:

The fair is crowded, and Ronnie walks along the crowd. Then she sees a beach volleyball tournament near the Wrightsville beach carnival, and wants to watch it. In the game, all the girls watch the handsome boys eagerly. Suddenly one player, who is handsome and popular, Will collide with her and spills her soda, and drenches her face, and shirt. After that, she meets, and befriends with a punker girl named Blaze. Then she sees Jonah coming through, and Jonah says that their father wants her to come, but Ronnie doesn't want, and does a deal with Jonah to hide Ronnie from Steve. Afterwards Blaze offers a dry shirt, and invites her to drink, and hang out with her friends. Then Blaze suggests going to a fireball act realized by her friend Marcus, who is the leader of the group, and Blaze's emotionally abusive boyfriend, on the pier. Next the police officer rushes through the fireball actors, and warns them. After they leave the place, Ronnie feels alone, and she goes after them.

## If I Were ...

***"The boys grabbed their coats and began moving up the pier, toward the carnival rides. Blaze followed, leaving Ronnie alone. Ronnie felt the officer's gaze on her, but she ignored him. Instead, she hesitated only briefly before going after them." pg. 37***

If I were Ronnie, I wouldn't go after them, because she has met with them only a few minutes ago, so she doesn't know them well. Consequently they can affect her dangerously, and unacceptably. Later she can be addicted to drugs, alcohols, and other addictive things by them, and be treated cruelly by them. I think she makes a wrong decision, but maybe she thinks that she can forget her father, and be an enjoyable summer time by joining this gang, so it can be an escape from Steve for Ronnie.

**<u>The Last Song</u>** **<u>27.01.10</u>**

**Chapter 4:**

**Questions about things that confuse me/wonder about:**

*"He'd known she would follow them." Pg. 38*

**1) Why does Ronnie follow the group even though she doesn't know them well?**

*"You'll talk to Blaze, but not me."*
*"I don't even know you."*
*"You don't know Blaze, either. You just met her." Pg. 39-40*

**2) Why doesn't Ronnie want to talk with Marcus even though she talks with Blaze?**

*Instead, he stared at Ronnie, liking the purple streak in her hair and her tight little body, the Glittery effect of her eye shadow. It was sort of an upscale, trampy style, despite the stupid shirt she was wearing. He liked that. He liked that a lot. (...)Marcus sauntered toward Ronnie and took a seat beside her. Close, but not too close. Blaze was the jealous type, and he didn't want her running Ronnie off before he had a chance to get to know her. (...) pg. 38-39*

*"I know a guy who's got a place down there just outside of Tampa. If you want, I'll bring you. We can stay there as long as you want. My car's over there." pg. 40*

**3) Will Ronnie and Marcus be lovers in the next chapters? *(I wonder if Ronnie will love Marcus, and they will be good friends.)***

**<u>The Last Song</u>** **<u>28.01.10</u>**

**Chapter 5:**

**Quotes/ Passages from the characters/book**

***No matter what he was doing, Will could always feel the weight of the secret pressing down on him. (...)He would see himself running up the beach and grabbing Scott as he stared at the raging fire.***
***What the hell did you do? he remembered screaming.***
***It's not my fault! Scott had screamed back.***
***It was only then, however, that Will realized they weren't alone. In the distance, he noticed Marcus, Blaze, Teddy, and Lance, watching them, and he knew at once they'd seen everything that happened. They knew... pg. 43***

***(...)It was one thing to cover for an accidental fire. Maybe he could have done that. But someone had been injured that night, and he felt a sickening surge of guilt whenever he drove by the site. It didn't matter that the church was being rebuilt or that the pastor had***

***long since been released from the hospital; what mattered was that he knew what had happened and hadn't done anything about it. Pg. 44***

I think that Will's best friend Scott lights the church ,and Will keeps it secretly in his depths, but he is afraid that Scott will be arrested, because probably Marcus, Teddy, Blaze see Scott, when he lights the church. Also it is dangerous, and harmful, because the fire hurts the pastor and harms the church. On the other hand, Will feels guilty, because he knows a lot of things about this fire, but he doesn't tell to someone.

***"The fight's over! There is no fight! Can't you see this kid is hurt?" pg. 52***
Ronnie says to the fighting two groups .

***"Are you okay, sweetie? Where's your mom? Let's go find her, okay?" pg. 52***
Ronnie says to the toddler.

She says them, when the two groups fight with each other, and one toddler loses its way. Then Ronnie sees it, and wants to protect it. I noticed that in this chapter Ronnie seems like a protective, lovely, and sensitive mother, because she helps the baby ,who starts walking, and loses its way, be by stopping the fight , because the toddler walks along the group members , and it can hurt. Then she takes it, and behaves in a pleasurable way. Afterwards she finds his mother, and brings it to her.

**My Feelings about the Character:**
**Will:** In this chapter, he is helpful, because he helps Ronnie's father to find Ronnie. Also he seems to me too complicated, and weary, because he doesn't know what he should do with his best friend Scott, who is the church arson, and with his ex-girl friend Ashley's behaviours, so his brain is mixed up. I think he is a quiet sensitive boy, because he rarely speaks, and answers back, when Ashley says something, he acts careless ,and often murmurs.

**The Last Song** **29.01.10**

**Chapter 6:**

**Quotes/ Passages from the characters/book**

Steve says to Ronnie:
***"Who's Marcus?"*** when police take Ronnie to home, and Steve waits for her. **pg. 59**

***"Good night, sweetheart," he called out. "I love you."*** when Ronnie goes to his horrible room, and Steve says good-bye to her. Then she is alone with her brother. **pg. 59**

***"Do you want breakfast? I made some bacon."*** when Ronnie wakes up, and grumbles about her room, and the shameful event. **pg. 64**

It shows that Steve wants to be more lovely, and he is concerned about his seventeen years old reluctant, depressive, rebellious, angry, and bitter daughter Ronnie, so he wants to know her friends, and where she goes. Also she wants to be nice by serving her a high-quality, and fine breakfast, and speaking with her gently.

***"I rode the Ferris wheel," Jonah said. "It was pretty cool to be so high. That's how Dad found you."***
***"It was awesome. Did you ride it?"*** **pg. 60**

Jonah says to Ronnie, when Ronnie goes to their room, and Jonah comes, and says to her that the room belongs to both of them. It shows that Jonah is a playful, and a funny boy, because he tells the things that he does in the fair eagerly, and wants to have fun, so in all chapters we can see his humours, and funny quotes.

**Jonah's Similar Quotes:**

***""I am, too. Mom and Ronnie fought the whole time."pg. 15***

***"Tell him you didn't see me."***
***Jonah thought about it. "Five bucks."***
***"What?"***
***"Gimme five bucks and I'll forget you were here."***
***"Are you serious?"***
***"You don't have much time," he said. "Now it's ten bucks."***
***(...) "You missed your chance. But your secret will be safe with me." pg.32***

Foreshadowing:

***Blaze shrugged, her expression <u>mischievous</u>, and Ronnie smiled. (...) "Do you have <u>any money?"</u> (...)"Why?" Blaze stood straight. "I haven't eaten since yesterday morning. I'm kind of hungry." pg. 66***

I can predict that Blaze will control Ronnie, and influence her to do wrong, and illegal things. Also Blaze will use Ronnie as a doll, so Ronnie will do unacceptable things, and Blaze's jobs for Blaze even though they met with each other just a few hours ago.

**The Last Song** **30.01.10**

**Chapter 7:**

**Foreshadowing:**

***The thing was, Will wasn't exactly sure why he was thinking about the girl. Particularly considering how little he knew about her. Yeah, she was pretty—he'd noticed that right off, despite the purple hair and dark mascara—but the beach was full of pretty girls. Nor was it the way she'd stopped the fight in its tracks. Instead, he kept coming back to the way she'd treated the little boy who'd fallen. He'd glimpsed a surprising tenderness beneath her rebellious exterior, and it had piqued his curiosity.***
***(...)Not all the time. But enough to make him realize that for whatever reason, he definitely wanted to get to know her a little better, and he found himself wondering whether he would see her again. pg.69***

I can say that in the next chapters they will be not just good friends, they will be affectionate ,and tender lovers, so in these passages the author wants to give us Will's first impression ,and emotions about Ronnie. Also we can understand that Will will start to be in Ronnie's side, and his heart will go out to Ronnie. Incidentally he wants to see her again, and speak with her as her friend.

**Quote from this chapter:**

***"Hey, by the way, did you see the girl who stopped the fight?" Will asked. "The one who helped the little boy find his mom?"(...) "You mean the vampire chick in the cartoon shirt?"***
***"She's not a vampire."-Will***
***"Yeah, I saw her. On the short side, ugly purple streak in her hair, black fingernail polish? You poured your soda over her, remember? She thought you smelled."***
***"What?"-Will***
***"I'm just saying," he said, (...) "You didn't notice her expression after you slammed Into her, but I did. She couldn't get away from you fast enough. Hence, you probably smelled."***
***"She had to buy a new shirt."***
***(...) "I don't know. She just surprised me. And I haven't seen her around here before."-Will pg.68-69***
(A conversation between Will and Scott, when they work with the oil drain in the Ford Explorer, and Scott starts to talk about the last night.)

It shows that Will defends, and supports Ronnie, and wants to learn more about Ronnie, so he asks to his best friend in a secret way, and he has sympathy for her. I think that it is a start of their relationship. It seems to me that Will will find her, because he always asks about her. Also it shows that the beginning of something for Will, starts with curiosity for Ronnie.

**The Last Song** **03.02.10**

**Chapter 8:**

Quote from this chapter:

***"We're having a little get-together at Bower's Point. Not just us. A bunch of people. I want you to come. Without the cops this time."* pg. 77**
(Marcus says to Ronnie, when they talk about their tonight's plans.)

I think that Marcus wants to be nice, friendly, and kind to Ronnie by inviting her to the party, so she can find new friends, and be better, and more satisfied, because she is new, and hasn't got many friends in the town. On the other hand, he may cooks up some plans to be with Ronnie, because he is in love with Ronnie, but she thinks that he is a weird, a little crazy , creepy and psychopathic boy, because when they are alone with Ronnie in the camp fire, he asks to her annoying questions ,and his behaviours are quick and strange. I think that he has got strange manners because he plays with the fire, so it isn't a normal hobby, and Ronnie is afraid of him because of his actions and the way of showing his feelings to Ronnie and his girlfriend Blaze.

**The Last Song** **03.02.10**

**Chapter 9:**

Questions about things that confuse me/wonder about:

*The frames were dusty, untouched in years. He knew that it had been his mother who put them there, and as he stared at them, he wondered what his father thought as he looked at them, or if he even saw them at all, or if he even realized they were there. pg.81*
**Why doesn't he touch, or look to his family photo?**

*"I know you how important that was to you"- Ronnie's mother pg. 81*

**Why is it important to Steve that his father says to him that he loves Steve?**

*As he took his seat at the piano, he felt it again, the same thing he'd told the marriage counsellor as he'd sat on the couch. He felt empty. pg.87*

**Why does Steve always feel empty even though he plays piano?**

Quote from this chapter:

***He wondered where she was and what she was doing. – Steve* pg. 79**

In this chapter, he seems like a concerned father, so he is worried about Ronnie, and considers in Rachel, and cares her. On the other hand, he can't articulate his feelings about her daughter, and besides he prefers playing piano, so sometimes Ronnie doesn't hear him, and goes to her way.

**The Last Song** **04.02.10**

**Chapter 10:**

Summary of this chapter:

Ronnie, Blaze, Marcus, and his group are at the beach party, and Marcus becomes interested in Ronnie, so he crushes on Ronnie. Then he starts to walk with her, and pulls her closer to him, but Ronnie doesn't want him, and often emphasizes her dissatisfaction. Afterwards Marcus wants to be over with Ronnie, but Ronnie refuses it. However after Marcus thanks her loudly for asking him to be her date, so he wants to show Ronnie as a girl, who steals her friend's boyfriend, to the people around the beach, especially Blaze. Afterwards Ronnie goes to his house, and her father asks some questions, and also gives her some food. Next day, she feels embarrassed, and guilty, and wants to find Blaze to tell her the truth. Then she finds her in the same music store that they often go. Slowly she looks at the CDs, and some of the collector's items pique her interest. After taking a breath, she starts to tell her the reality, but Blaze doesn't believe her. Secretly Blaze sets Ronnie up when they are both in a record store. She slips valuable records in Ronnie's tote bag, and Ronnie is caught for shoplifting.

**The Last Song** **06.02.10**

**Chapter 11:**

Quotes from this chapter:

***"Ronnie said she didn't want to see the piano."***
***"There's no place to hide the piano, so I put a wall up instead. Now she doesn't have to see it." pg.99***
***(...)He thought again about the years he'd lost and would never get back. –Steve pg.107***
(He says it to Jonah, when they build a wall between the piano and the main room.)

Steve is a sensitive and concerned man, so he understands Ronnie's feelings, and wants to be closer to Ronnie. He respects to her choices, so Ronnie doesn't want to see piano every single day, and Steve finds a way to hide it. When he hides it, Ronnie will not be so angry to Steve, and maybe she forgets the old days, so it is a wonderful change to have good relationship like father-daughter between them. With this way, they can fix this problems between them, and their relationship can get back to normal and proper.

***"Oh," Jonah said, thinking. "You know, I really don't like having to do homework. In fact, I don't even like to see it piled on my desk." (...) "I'm just saying that maybe I should build a wall around the desk in my room." –Jonah pg.99***
(He says it to Steve, when they build a wall between the piano and the main room.)

***"You said we were going to go kite flying."***
***(...) "Okay. But then we're going to fly the kite, right?"***
***(...) "All afternoon?" –Jonah pg.99***

He is a funny boy, so he can always be cheerful and enthusiastic. Also he wants to play and have fun, and often uses his sense of humour in bad situations or for criticizing Ronnie. For example, he says "I am, too. Mom and Ronnie fought the whole time." to his father, when they come to the Steve's house at the first time, so it shows that he criticizes Ronnie ,and accuses her for disturbing him. Another example, he says "(...) And Ronnie doesn't always come with us. She locks herself in her room and refuses to come out, but as soon as we leave, she goes over to Starbucks to hang out with her friends. It makes Mom furious." To his dad, when they make stained-glass for the rebuilding church, so it shows that he makes fun of Ronnie in an indirect way, and he seems like a trustworthy boy who says everything without using any guile.

***"I don't want anything to happen to the turtle eggs tonight." –Ronnie pg.106***
(She says it to her father, when they look to the sea turtles near their house on the beach. Then her father talks about the turtle eggs, which are in danger, so they must protect them by waiting near it.)

She seems like a sensitive, understanding and protective girl. Also her feelings start to change in this chapter gradually. Besides protecting the sea turtles, her relationship with her father gets better, and they start talking about her feelings and the events which is important for Ronnie. Also we can understand that Ronnie becomes calmer, more sensitive and kinder in the later chapters by looking her behaviours and sayings in this chapter.

**Foreshadowing:**

***It was the first time since she'd been here that she'd spoken to him without a hint of anger or frustration. pg.104***
***In profile, he could see both the young woman she was becoming and the little girl he remembered.*** **pg. 105**

I will predict that she will mature gradually, and change her characteristics, so her angry, grouchy, horrible and unlike characteristics will change into calm, lovely, compassionate, sympathetic, satisfied, sensitive, helpful and friendly behaviours. Also gradually her relationship with his father will develop and be better, so they understand each other and have sympathy to each other. Besides this, they can speak with each other friendly, and be close to each other. I think that love will change her, and she will be a young woman with a gold heart.

**The Last Song 07.02.10**

**Chapter 12:**

**Foreshadowing:**

***"(...) the man was closer and hunting around the dune. She started toward him, wondering what he was doing, and then he turned in her direction. When their eyes met, it was one of the few times in her life that she actually felt tongue-tied." pg.110***

The man is Will and they see each other at the first time. Then they will hang out together as lovers, because according to this paragraph Ronnie feels tongue-tied, so it happens when you love someone, and you can't say anything, and mumble something because of your nerves and you feel the presence of love in your heart.

***Leaning over, and for the first time in three years, she kissed him on the cheek. "Good night, Dad."* pg. 122**

Their relationship will get nicer and better, so we can understand that Ronnie's attitudes will change, because she are in love ,and it will also change her feelings to another people. Also she will be more friendly, nice and lovely, and she will love to stay in there with her father. Besides this, she will learn to respect to her father, and she will start to give him her love and interest which hasn't been given by her to him for three years.

**Quotes from this chapter:**

***"This isn't normal," he said. "Someone should be mad. Someone's always mad in the mornings."***
***"Are you talking about me?" Ronnie asked. She put two Pop-Tarts in the toaster. "I'm always cheerful." pg.115***
( Jonah and Ronnie speak with each other, when they start eating the breakfast after Ronnie's night on the beach.)

It shows that Ronnie changes, and she is more cheerful, so she likes this place. I think because of her love she is so satisfied, and in this chapter Jonah is also surprised, because of the maturity and happiness of Ronnie. On the other hand, in other chapters she argues with Jonah, her mother and Steve, and always criticizes the beach, food and Steve's old and diminutive house, so she seems like a bad-tempered girl, but she grows up and her feelings change. Also she shows this change with her gestures.

**My Feelings about Characters:**

**Ronnie:** In the first part of this chapter, she is too nervous and worried, because she is arrested for shoplifting even though she is innocence, so when her mother learns this, she can give her grounds, and Ronnie doesn't want her mother to learn her misunderstood shoplifting, but gradually she gets calmer, because she sees Will, who spills soda to her, and her heart starts experiencing a different emotion called "LOVE", when she sees him at the first time on the beach. Also she feels tongue-tied, but she isn't sure about her feelings ,and she wants to keep her distance with Will. After she gets more cheerful ,and I think it is a result of being in love. Besides her satisfaction, she becomes protective, so she starts to protect the sea turtles from being eaten by raccoons by sleeping near their nests all the night and protecting them.

**Steve:** In this chapter, he wants to fix his relationship with his daughter, so he doesn't say Ronnie's shoplifting to his ex-wife, and he prepares a vegetarian breakfast to her. Besides this, he buys coffee, and asks to her if she wants coffee or not. After his efforts, Ronnie kisses him on the cheek and wants to be nice to him.

**The Last Song** **08.02.10**

**Chapter 13:**

**Foreshadowing:**

***But when she turned, smiling as she waved a final good night from the porch, he felt something leap inside at the notion that she just might imagine it was the beginning of something, too. Pg. 134***
***(...)He laughed before catching her eye. She looked down at the sand, then up the beach, then finally toward him. She shook her head, unable to suppress a smile, as if marveling at what was happening between them and enjoying every moment.pg. 146***

They will have a relationship, but they will not just good friends, so they will be lovers. According to these passages from this chapter, I can say that it starts something new ,and they want to be together, so when their eyes meet it happens something ,and something makes them feel enjoyable, so I think it is love, and they will find it in the next chapters.

**Quotes from this chapter:**

***"You stopped the fight, even though everyone else wanted blood. You were the only one who even noticed the kid who started to cry, and I saw the way you smiled when he went off with his mom. You read Tolstoy in your spare time. And you like sea turtles."pg.136***
( Will says it to Ronnie, when Ronnie wants to protect the sea turtles by sleeping over the night near their nest ,and then Will comes ,and wants to join to her, because he says that she can be hurted, but after Jonnie is angry with him, because he says to her father where Ronnie and her new friends go, and her father comes to take her, so she feels embarrassed in front of her new friends. )

Will wants to reassure and convince her that they have got many common points. I think that Will tries to tell why he loves Ronnie ,and what are some of the reasons which make Will feel sympathy for Ronnie . Besides this, he emphasizes the similarities between him and Ronnie. For example, both of them love and care about the sea turtles, and are sensitive. Also he loves Tolstoy too, so when she reads the book, he says that he read it, and gives one quote from the book. According to this quote, Will wants to be with her, and doesn't want a small event like previous to prevent their relationship.

***"Just keep doing what you're doing," he encouraged. Pg. 141***
( Will says it to Ronnie, when they go fishing ,and Ronnie can't learn it well, and makes many mistakes by fishing and pulling the hook.)

It shows that Will is a helpful ,reassuring and encouraging person, so he tries to teach fishing to Ronnie again and again, and sometimes he pulls it, so Ronnie can see ,and makes what he does. Then he gives her commands ,and Ronnie reels. Also with help of Will, Ronnie eventually achieves to fish something. Besides fishing, they have fun together ,and without Will's help and reassurance, she can't be so successful ,and without Will, she can't be so cheerful.

***"It's not me you should be worried about. There are bad people everywhere. Even here."***

***(…) "If it came down to that, I'd protect you in a heartbeat." Pg. 129***
(Will says it to Ronnie, when he sees her in the public beach by reading her book ,and sleeping there for protecting the sea turtles nests. Then Will comes, and similarly he wants to sleep there. )

Will seems like a protective person in this chapter ,and he wants to defend her, so it shows that he cares her so much, and although sleeping on the sand in the night is cold, dark, itchy, frightened and awful, he joins to her, and doesn't leave her alone.

**<u>The Last Song 10.02.10</u>**

**Chapter 14:**

**Passage from the chapter:**

***After winking at Ronnie, he readied himself for the next shot. pg.148***

It shows that when Will thinks about Ronnie, he knows that she always supports him ,and he becomes more calm, cheerful, energetic ,and full of pride,so he motives himself ,and is ready for everything, because he know that their love, synergy and happiness can face any problems, and at the end they win and beat all of them. According to this passage, Ronnie seems like an inspiration for Will,so when he looks at her,she makes him encouraged to be as good and successful as possible.

**If I Were …**

***"Uh-huh," Ronnie said again, trying to sound noncommittal. (…)This time, Ronnie couldn't mask her surprise. (…) Ronnie stared at her in disbelief, feeling the world around her suddenly begin to narrow. (…) Ronnie felt the blood drain from her face. She told herself not to listen, not to believe it, that Will wasn't that way. But the words kept echoing in her mind… pg.149***
***"Please don't make me stay. I don't like it here. I don't like the people here. I don't fit in here. I don't belong here. I want to go home." Her dad said nothing, but she saw the disappointment in his face. pg.151***
***"I thought you were different. I just thought…" He stared at her, his face a mixture of anger and disappointment (…) pg.158***

If I were Ronnie, I wouldn't believe Ashley, because she is Will's last girlfriend, and she lies to her. Besides that, Ronnie doesn't follow her heart, because Will and she spend a lot of time

,and Ronnie knows that Will loves her intensively, so I think that he can't lie to her ,and Will thinks that Ronnie has got many similarities with him. For example, both of them love the sea turtles and all kind of sea animals, so Will shows to her a loggerhead which isn't showed to the public. In my opinion, she makes a wrong decision, and it seems to me that she will miss him a lot in the next chapters, and I hope that she will believe to him again, so they will be again a credible pair.

Foreshadowing:

**Without thinking, Ronnie walked toward him and felt him hold her close. There was something... gentle and forgiving in his embrace, something she'd missed for years. It was all she could do to stop the tears from coming before she pulled back. Pg.154**

It's a little dream, after Ashley says that Will tricks her. Also Ronnie believes him in her depths, but she isn't sure. However I think that eventually she will believe him ,and they will continue to their relationship. Besides that, she will miss him so much ,and want him to be with her. According to her little dream, she thinks a scene that Will holds her close to him as they are still lovers ,and she feels something that connects them together. It is a strange feeling that she only lives with his reassuring embrace.

Questions about things that confuse me/wonder about:

*"She turned away, angry at him, but even angrier at herself for being so stupid." pg.150*
**Why does Ronnie believe to Ashley ?**

*There was something... gentle and forgiving in his embrace, something she'd missed for years. Pg.154*
**Why doesn't he want to talk with Will even though she believes him?**

*"I thought you were different. I just thought..." He stared at her, his face a mixture of anger and disappointment (...) pg.158*
**Why doesn't Ronnie tell him what Ashley says to her about Will?**

**The Last Song** **11.02.10**

**Chapter 15:**

Questions about things that confuse me/wonder about:

*"Didn't you hear me?" he snarled. "Do you ever listen to a single thing I say? I said I'm not hungry." pg.160*

**Why is Marcus angry to Blaze?**

*"Come here," he said. He forced a smile. "Sit next to me. I don't want you to go just yet." pg.162*

**Why does Marcus want her even though he doesn't like her? What is his plans ?**

*It was the perfect solution to get Ronnie to keep her distance... which meant that Marcus wouldn't have a chance to see Ronnie either. pg.160*

**Does he want to see Ronnie again? / Does he make plans to get Ronnie back?**

*He liked the fact that he could scare her. He could use it to his advantage. pg.162*

**How can Marcus use this advantage in the next chapter?**

*No one did that to him. Especially girls. Who in the hell did she think she was? Tight little body or not, he didn't like it. He didn't like it at all. pg.162*

**Does Marcus want Ronnie even though she doesn't care him and her body language signals angry defiance?**

**The Last Song 11.02.10**

**Chapter 16:**

**My Feeling About the Character :**

**Steve:** In this chapter, there are a lot of flashbacks to his childhood, and when he is in Ronnie's age, he asks questions about the God, and Pastor Harris gives answers to him, and in one of their conversation he says that he hasn't got any friends to talk, and Pastor Harris teaches him listening his heart Also he says that all the answers are in the heart, but the only difficulty is to hear it. I think that Steve is a little religious person. For example he reads Bible in his free times. Besides that, he thinks about his old times that he is a teacher, and he always gives good, and useful advices to the children. Then the parents thank to him about the reasonable advices. On the other hand, he can't give this kind of advices to his own daughter.

**The Last Song 12.02.10**

**Chapter 17:**

Quotes from this chapter:

***"After I stopped teaching at Juilliard, I did every show that I could. It was my dream, you know? Be a famous concert pianist? Anyway... I guess I should have thought more about the reality of the situation before I made the decision. But I didn't. I didn't realize how hard it was going to be on your mom." (...)"In the end, we just sort of... drifted apart." pg.179***
(Steve tells it to Ronnie, when Ronnie wants to learn why her father and mother divorces.)

It shows that Steve is regretful, and understands that he only thinks himself, so he decides something, without thinking about his wife and especially his family,because his decisions can affect them,so he must think of that. Besides his regret, it is a moment that Ronnie and he can speak together ,and share their ideas, problems and mistakes with a honest and lovely way. It is the first time that Ronnie feels sympathy for his father ,and wants to understand him by asking questions about him, so she can learn how he feels, thinks ,and behaves.

***"What am I going to do?" -Ronnie***
***"You mean about today?"- Steve***
***"I mean about everything."-Ronnie pg.180***
(Ronnie says it to Steve, after his father tells her about his divorce with her mother.)

It seems to me that she wants to hear some advices, but Steve is the last person who gives advices to her, because she doesn't care him in other chapters. I think that she needs to ask him. There are several reasons for this. First of all, she hasn't got a lot friends in this place, so she can't ask to them ,and talk about her situation. Other one is he wants to be nice to her ,and does everything she thinks or likes. Finally a lot of complicated events happen in her life ,and everything happens fast and consecutively, so she hasn't got any chance ,because she must tell someone ,and let off steam ,and takes advices.

**The Last Song** **14.01.10**

**Chapter 18:**

Questions about things that confuse me/wonder about:

*"Yeah. What was that about? Yesterday, you spent your whole day off with her, and then she shows up this morning and you kiss her? Are you, like... serious about her or something?" Will remained silent. pg.190*

**Is Will really serious with Ronnie?**

*"See, here's the thing. The last thing you need is to get serious with a girl. You need to concentrate on what's important. You've got a full-time job, you volunteer trying to save the dolphins or whales or turtles or whatever, and you know how much we have to practice to get ready for the tournament. You don't have enough time as it is!"*
*(...) You're going to turn into a hermit. You're going to blow off your friends so you can hang out with her. Trust me, the last thing you need is to get serious with... pg.190-191*

**Does Will do what Scot says to him? /Does he continue their relationship with Ronnie?**

<u>**The Last Song**</u> **27.02.10**

**Chapter 19:**

**Quotes/Passages from this chapter:**

***"You didn't tell me your last name was Blakelee," Ronnie mumbled. Pg.195***
***"You didn't ask." He gave an indifferent shrug. "Come on in." Pg.195***

Ronnie says it to Will, when Will takes her to his enormous and splendid house, and Ronnie sees the small brass "The Blakelees" plaque posted near the door. It shows us that Will doesn't want Ronnie to be with him because of money, or think that he is only a snob. However, he is kind, bashful, obedient, and compassionate and sympathetic even though his family is enormous rich. On the other hand, he may want to be known with his name not his family name.

**Similar Passage:**
**He loved his dad and his family name, and he was proud of the business his dad had built. He appreciated the advantages that his life had brought him, but... he wanted to be his own person, too. He wanted people to know him first as *Will,* not *Will Blakelee (...) pg. 207***

**Though Susan tried to hide it, Ronnie could tell she wasn't pleased about having been surprised by Will's unexpected guest. (...)Though Ronnie felt like telling him to *hurry,* she didn't. "Okay," she offered instead. Pg. 196 The woman had made it abundantly clear that she either didn't like Ronnie or didn't like the fact that her son liked Ronnie. Pg. 203**
(When Ronnie waits in front of his house for Will to clean himself ,and his mother Susan looks them carefully.)

It is Ronnie's first impression about Will's mother, and she doesn't like Ronnie, so it can affect their relationship with Will. Also his mother may complains a lot about hanging out with Ronnie, and she can be an obstacle to them, because it is important to be loved and accepted by his/her family to his/her family ,when you are in love with someone, so negative and undesirable impression can cause a lot of serious and critical problems for a serious relationship.

**Similar Quotes/Passages:**
**As she struggled playfully with him, she noticed Susan watching from the veranda. From the expression on her face, she was definitely not happy. Pg. 216 "It will if your mom finds out. I'm pretty sure she doesn't like me."**
**"Why do you say that?"**
***Because I saw the way she was looking at me earlier,* she could have said. "It's just a feeling." Pg. 218**
*(Second impression, and she still doesn't like their continuous relationship)*

**"Don't be embarrassed." (...) "He gets embarrassed a lot. He used to be the shyest kid in the world. He couldn't even sit near a pretty girl without his cheeks turning bright red." Will, meanwhile, was shaking his head in disbelief. "I can't believe you're saying this, Dad. Right in front of her." Pg. 199**

Will's father says it to Ronnie, when Ronnie is in Will's house waiting for Will, and his father takes her to his airplane collection room. It is difficult to think that Will used to be shy, because he has got a lot of friends especially two or more girlfriends, and goes many parties. Also I think that his father mustn't say this, because everyone gets mortified especially in front of his/her friends .

**"Listen to me. Even if they serve you eggplant on rutabaga with tofu, I want you to eat what they put in front of you and then make sure you compliment them on the meal," Tom admonished. (...)"Don't be sorry. I like him." pg. 200**

Will's father says it to Will, when Ronnie and Will starts going to Ronnie's house for meeting with her family particularly with her father and having dinner. From this quote we see that his father is a kind man even though they are too prosperous, so some rich people can be arrogant and smug, because they think that money can buy everything, and control people. On the other hand , Will is generous and kind as well, so we can say that our behaviors are effected by our families. Also our behaviors reflect what we learn and see in our family. Besides that, Will's family's behaviors make him different and than other conceited and snobbish people and they make Ronnie be in love with him.

**(...) it was the first time she'd ever brought a boy to meet her father. Would he try to give them space by hiding out in the kitchen? Would he try to become buddies with Will? Would he do or say something that embarrassed her?(...) she'd already begun thinking of escape plans she could use as soon as they finished dinner. Pg. 201**

Ronnie thinks it, when she and Will are in his truck going to her house. It's clear that Ronnie is too nervous and anxious because of her father. She doesn't know what he will do, and she is afraid that he will embarrass her like Will's father does by talking about the old days. However I think that Ronnie and her father don't spend much time together in the past, and he will be careful when he says and does something, because he really loves her and doesn't want to lose her in their gorgeous and superb summer that they spend together as really daughter-father, but it is normal for Ronnie to think of those things, because she really loves Will ,and wants to create a terrific and glorious impression.

**As for Will, he was just the kind of guy her mom wanted Ronnie to date: polite, respectful, intelligent, and best of all, sans tattoos... pg. 202 Her dad would do none of those things—he seemed to trust Ronnie's judgment and was content to let her make her own decisions without inserting his own opinions. Pg. 202- 203**

She thinks it, when Will comes to meet with her family to dinner. It shows us that her mother seems like an authoritative person, so she always interferes Ronnie's relationships. Also she doesn't trust Ronnie's opinions and individual judgements, and wants to control her. On the other hand, his father seems like a nice and understanding person, and trusts her even though when she is arrested for shoplifting ,and whereas her mother says that she can go to the jail in New York at the first time they come to his house.

**<u>The Last Song</u>** **<u>27.02.10</u>**

**Chapter 20:**

Quotes/Passages from this chapter:

**(...) The thought that this was the girl with whom he'd like to face the future. Pg. 204 (...)He knew Scott wouldn't understand the concept—Scott seemed unable to imagine a future that stretched past the upcoming weekend—but then Scott wasn't so different from most of his peers. (...)He wasn't into one-night stands, he wasn't into scoring to see if he could,(...) When he met a girl, the first question he asked himself wasn't whether she was good for a few dates; it was whether she was the kind of girl he could imagine spending time with over the long haul. Pg. 205**

Will thinks it, when he walks with Ronnie after the dinner with Ronnie's family. I think that he wants to a partner who devotes him. Also he wants both Will and his girlfriend to be devoted and loyal, and permanent relationships and marriages are important for him. Besides this, he doesn't understand Scott's attitude towards friendship and marriage, because Scott always says to Will that he must date with Ashley because of fun, so Will gets angry with Scott ,and doesn't want to hear Scott's conversation about friendship and Ashley.

**Through it all, they had loved each other well, celebrating their successes and supporting each other during tragedy. Neither of them was perfect, but he'd grown up certain that they were a team, and eventually, he'd absorbed that lesson. Pg. 205**

Will thinks his parents' marriage, when he walks with Ronnie on the beach. It's clear that he thinks that his family is an impressive model for him about relationship and marriage, because they always support each other like a team, and stick with each other in good and bad times, so we can say that they are passionate and faithful, and their marriage seem eternal to Will. Also he wants to have both love and passion like their parents have.

My Feelings About The Events:

**She wasn't like anyone he'd met before. He was sure he wanted never to let go of her hand; their fingers seemed to fit together in just the right way—effortlessly clasped, like perfect complements. (...)when he looked up, he caught the brief flash of a shooting star passing overhead. When he turned to Ronnie, he knew by her expression that she'd seen it as well. "What did you wish for?" she asked, her voice a whisper. But he couldn't answer. Instead, he raised her hand and slipped his other arm around her back. He stared at her, knowing with certainty that he was falling in love. He pulled her close and kissed her beneath a blanket of stars, wondering how on earth he'd been lucky enough to find her. Pg. 213**

I think that Will wishes to have a permanent bond like his parents, and wants to never let Ronnie go, so he wants to stick her in her bad or good times, and I feel that they will be in love until the end. Also in this part they understand each other, and what they will do. I believe that nothing can separate them such as Ashley, Will's mother and the end of the summer, because many summer loves don't continue much time, and it is called "summer fling". However I want them to continue their love, because they complement each other like water and flower. For example, after Ronnie falls in love with him, she becomes more lovely and compassionate. I can stress that after this moment they should hold each other tightly.

**The Last Song** **27.02.10**

**Chapter 21:**

Quote from this chapter:

**And I'd be willing to bet that you were great at it, if only because you have to love something before you can hate it." Pg. 219**
**"It's not my business, but if you were that good, then you're only hurting yourself. It's a gift, right? And who knows? Maybe you could go to Juilliard."(...) She heard the sincerity in his tone and knew he meant what he'd said. Pg. 220**

Will says it to Ronnie, when they are in front of Will's house and play and make fun together. From this quote we see that Will seems like a perceptive boy, and understands her feelings and situation, so he gives advices by analyzing her situation. It is important for their relationship, so a good boyfriend or husband should have these qualities. Also he should be observant, understanding and sympathetic. Besides this, in previous chapters he rarely gives advice or shows and explains his feelings about Ronnie's situation, so he only thinks their situation and feelings, but he wants to be sure about both their feelings and development of their love.

**The Last Song** **28.02.10**

**Chapter 22:**

My Feelings About The Events:
**He remembered setting fire to a barn when he was twelve and watching it burn for hours, thinking he'd never seen anything more incredible. So he'd lit another one, this time at an abandoned warehouse. Over the years, he'd set a bunch of them. There was nothing better; nothing made him higher than the power he felt with a lighter in his hands. Pg. 222**

I think that Marcus' childhood is the beginning of his attitudes and problems, because if he doesn't watch and set fire in his childhood, he doesn't be so mean and weird, and harm people such as Blaze, Ronnie, Will, and Scott. He controls Blaze, and dates with her only for the money that she earns. Also Marcus ruins Megan's wedding and causes problems between Will's mother and Ronnie, because Susan thinks that Marcus comes to the wedding secretly because of Ronnie. In addition, because of his lies, Blaze gets jealous, and tricks Ronnie by putting a valuable record to Ronnie's bag, so Ronnie seems like a shoplifter.

**The Last Song** **28.02.10**

**Chapter 23:**

Quotes/Passages from this chapter:

**(...) he admitted that he sometimes resented the fact that he felt a responsibility to be the kind of person his mom insisted he be. Pg. 225**
**(...) he seemed to trust Ronnie's judgment and was content to let her make her own decisions without inserting his own opinions. Pg. 202-203**

It shows us that Will's mother always wants to controls him ,and when his mother says something, he mostly makes it or believes it. However I think that his mother wants to protect him especially after his brother's dead, but she seems like an overprotective mother, because she interferes in his decisions and thoughts. Also she wants to form and create his life and relationships. Unlike Susan, Steve always wants Ronnie to make her own decisions, and trusts and believes her. Besides this, he listens her without interruption. Also he respects her ,and thinks that she can decide what is good or appropriate for her. Moreover, he gives her a chance to find her own way even though she makes mistakes ,and sometimes goes to wrong ways.

**(...) the only blemish on their largely idyllic summer was the continuing presence of Marcus. (...) Will felt paralyzed. If he overreacted, Marcus might go to the police; if he did nothing, he felt ashamed. Pg. 227**

This proves that Will aren't sure what he have to do, so when he hits or harms Marcus, he tells the church fire's arsonist is Scott ,and it can affect Ronnie's shoplift problem. If he keep his anger inside, it makes him feel ashamed, because Marcus aggravates them on the beach ,and when he doesn't react in front of Ronnie, he feels useless and helpless, but his reaction can cause a lot of problems for their blissful love.

My Feelings About The Events:

**"Do you ever wonder what it means to be a friend?" "I'm not sure what you mean." (...) "How far would you go to protect a friend?" She hesitated. "I suppose that depends on what the friend did. And how serious it was." (...)"In the end, you should always do the right thing, even if it's hard. I know that might not help you and that the right thing isn't always so easy to figure out. At least on the surface, anyway. But even when I was justifying to myself that stealing was no big deal, I knew it was wrong. It was making me feel... dark inside." Pg. 233-234**

I think that Will secretly wants to emphasise Scott's fire accident. Also he wants to say that he protects Scott, because they are best friends ,and as a best friend it is necessary to support each other even though you don't feel comfortable or don't accept his/her mistake or false. You must cover it like Will does, so you should do something for his/her benefit even though it is hard to do. However I believe that he does the wrong thing, because every time when he sees or reads or hears about it, he gets angry, nervous and worried ,so it is better to say what Scott does instead of becoming on edge and annoyed. I feel that he tells this to her, because he may want to explain Scott's mistake.

**The Last Song 28.02.10**

**Chapter 24:**

My Feelings About The Events:

**"That. Was. So. Gross." (...)"Watching you and Will. Like I said, that was really gross."(...) "It was kind of hard not to. You were right there by the workshop with Will. It looked like he was practically squishing you to death." (...) "You'll understand when you're a little**

**older." Jonah shook his head. "I understand exactly what you were doing. I've seen movies. I just think it's gross." Pg.237**

Jonah says it Ronnie, when she comes to home in the evening, and sees Jonah watching them. It's clear that Jonah exaggerates things such as kissing in a funny and humorous way, but it is normal for his age to think like that, and he describes their action like Will pressing her to death. Then he answers back with a witty attitude. However his reaction and expression makes me laugh, and I think his sense of humour and amusing behaviours make the book more enjoyable, because his sarcastic way of speaking and telling the realities particularly about Ronnie makes me think about my funny brother. Similarly he always complains, and criticizes us by using amusing phrases and sentences.

**Similar Quotes/Passages:**
**"Oh, by the way, you owe me ten bucks."**
**"For what?"**
**"Hello? For not telling Dad about what Will and you were doing. Duh."**
**"Are you serious? Even though I'm going to make you dinner?"**
**"Come on. You work and I'm poor." Pg. 239-240** *( Again he is sarcastic and humorous.)*

**"I think we've all changed a lot this summer." "Yeah," he said. "I think I've gotten taller, for one thing." "You definitely have. And you've learned how to make a stained-glass window." (...)"I think I want to learn to stand on my head." Pg. 245**

**"You're getting married?"**
**"Of course not. Will's sister is getting married."(...)"Do you want to go?" Jonah asked curiously. "Will wants me to go. It's important to him. And it would be something to see." Pg. 254**

**(...)she didn't recognize the song. It seemed almost contemporary, unlike the music he usually played, but even to her ears it sounded... unfinished somehow. Her dad seemed to realize the same thing because he stopped for a moment, appeared to think of something new, and started over from the beginning. Pg. 241**

I feel that his song can be for his daughter, because she feels that it is so modern and different than his previous songs, so I believe that he doesn't write a kind of song that he doesn't know well, because he always plays and composes classical songs, but he never writes an up-to-date song as she states. However people can make different and special things to their family members or best friends who are unique in their lives.

Foreshadowing:
**As he played, he coughed once, then again, *before stopping the song*. He coughed some more, the sound thick and mucousy, and when it *continued unabated*, she broke into a run to reach him. "Dad?" she cried. "Are you okay?" pg. 241**
**(...) she was struck by how tired and frail he looked. (...) pg. 243**

I predict that her father will get sick ,and it will be really serious, because his coughing doesn't stop and continue some more. Also he looks so tired and weak, so these are the symptoms of a severe illness, and she will help him by spending time together, so she will motivate him by doing special things and care about him, but if he will die, she really will be grief. Besides this, she may start playing piano because of her father's illness, and his father will not stop playing piano even though he is sick.

<u>**The Last Song 06.03.10**</u>

**Chapter 26:**

My Feelings About The Events:

**Her comment made Ronnie think about the similarities in their lives—divorce, anger, and rebellion, a parent's remarriage—yet despite those things, they were no longer the same at all. Blaze had changed since the beginning of the summer. Gone was the zest for life Ronnie had noticed when they first met, and Blaze seemed older, too, as if she'd aged years instead of weeks. But not in a good way. There were bags under her eyes, and her skin was sallow. She'd lost weight, too. A lot of weight. In a strange way, it was as if Ronnie were seeing the person she might have become, and she didn't like what she saw. Pg. 250-251**

**"I don't have anywhere else to go. My mom called all the relatives and told them not to take me in. She told them that it's hard for her, but what I need is 'tough love' right now. But I don't have any money to eat, and unless I want to sleep on the beach every night for the rest of my life, I have to do what Marcus tells me. When he's mad at me, he won't even let me shower at his place. And he won't give me any money from the shows we do, so I can't eat, either. He treats me like a dog sometimes, and I hate it. But who else do I have?" pg. 251**

**For an instant, Ronnie thought she saw not only a flash of gratitude, but something that reminded her of the smart, lively girl she'd first met in June. pg. 252**

I think that Marcus really controls her ,and this causes her a lot of problems in her physical appearance, so that she seems to get older. However I think Blaze is still Ronnie's friend even though she tricks her , because Ronnie learns how to forgive people ,and how to be a good friend even though she sometimes joins to a wrong crowd such as Marcus' group consisting of his fire jugglers. Besides this, Ronnie seems like a protective and supportive friend, because she is friendly, welcoming, and generous to her visitor Blaze, and Blaze's attitudes and behaviours are reminded her the first time she sees her, because Blaze is now released from Marcus, so Marcus makes her more fragile, because he always gives her jobs and wants her to earn as much money as she can. Also because of this hard work, she gets tired ,and at the end she feels to be treated like a dog ,and escapes .

**"I'll bet the judge is setting her straight, though, huh?" *The judge…* Suddenly, Ronnie knew why the older man had looked so familiar… and now the judge was talking to Susan… She felt her own breath catch in her throat. Oh… God… pg. 269**

**"She ruined your sister's wedding!" "No, she didn't!" Will shouted back.**

**(…) It had to have something to do with that girl! (…)The way she said "that girl" made Ronnie sound like something disgusting(…)"You knew what was going to happen if you brought her here. You know she's not like us… "You haven't even given her a chance—"" Pg. 270**

**"Will, honey... don't you get that she's not good enough for you? You've got your whole future ahead of you, and the last thing you need in your life is someone like her. I've been waiting for you to figure it out on your own, but obviously you're too emotionally involved to see the obvious. She's not good enough for you. She's low-class. Low! Class!" (...)She didn't belong here. pg. 271**

I feel that Will's mother is prejudiced, because she judges Ronnie without knowing her well. Also she doesn't give a chance to Ronnie to meet with her, so her attitudes in her daughter's wedding isn't appropriate, and I think that separating people into groups such as poor-rich and popular-unpopular is humiliating and diabolical. Even though she says these disgusting things, I think her overprotective attitudes towards Will cause this, because after her son died in an accident, she thinks that it is only her fault ,and wants to protect her other children carefully. Besides this, Will also wants to protect Ronnie ,and doesn't want her mother to be so mean to her ,and wants her to give Ronnie a chance to introduce herself. However I believe that everyone can love whoever she/he wants, because love isn't depend on such wrong judgements about people's situations.

**"I mean, I'm glad Will invited you to the wedding. You should have your fun now because it's not going to last. He leaves in a couple of weeks. Have you thought about that yet?" (...)"Even if you two make plans to see each other, do you honestly think Will's mom is ever going to accept you?" Ashley went on. "Megan was engaged twice before this, and her mom ran both of them off. And she's going to do the same to you whether you like it or not. But even if she doesn't, you're leaving and he's leaving and it's not going to last." Pg.264**
**"I'm getting sick and tired of listening to your crap, so if you ever try to talk to me again, I'm going to punch those bleached teeth right out of your mouth. Got it?" pg.265**

I think that Ronnie reacts right, because Ashley is always an obstacle between them. In earlier chapters, she also wants them to break up, and tells to her a lot of false ideas and reasons why Will loves her ,and things like her last relationship with Will. However this time Ronnie doesn't believe her ,and I should say that her last word shows my feelings and reactions towards Ashley, so she says the exactly correct last sentence to her. Besides this, I think that Ashley should go to her own way ,and find a new so-called boyfriend.

**Quotes/Passages from this chapter:**

**"Then why don't you buy a gown?"**
**"Because I don't have any money," she said.**
**(...)"This one was for not telling Dad I saw you that night at the carnival." He pointed to a single. "This one was for not telling Dad that you were making out with Will." He continued to point at various bills. "This one was for the guy with blue hair, and this was from liar's poker. This one was for that time you snuck out after your curfew—"**
**(...) "So I don't really need it. And I like Will. He makes you happy."**
**Yeah, she thought, he does. "You're a pretty good little brother, you know?" pg.255**
**Mom needs me to cry, but Dad needs me to explain why I deserve it." Pg.255**

Conversation between Jonah and Ronnie, when she can't decide what she will wear for Will's sister's wedding. From this quote we learn that Jonah seems helpful for the first time, so he wants to give his money which is earned from blackmail, so he tricks his whole family members, and takes their money by using different methods. Also it can show us that he is very clever and cunning. Besides that, he shows us his support for his sister even though he earns his money from her ,and doesn't like her so much at the beginning, but I think that because of the changes in Ronnie's behaviours and attitudes towards him make him give his money to her.

**Add in the guests—she'd never seen so many tuxedos and formal gowns in her life—and she couldn't help but feel out of place already. She really didn't belong here. Pg.258**
**For a long time, all he could do was stare at her. In the extended silence, the butterflies in her stomach began to feel like birds, and all she could think was that she'd done something wrong. Maybe she'd arrived too early, or maybe she'd overdone it with her dress and makeup.pg.259 (...) Will seemed content to fix his eyes on Ronnie from his spot near the trellis. Pg. 260**

Ronnie thinks the guests, when she comes to Will's sister's wedding. It shows us that she feels worried and preoccupied, because it is her first time that she sees a wedding like this, so everybody wears expensive , elegant and handy tuxedos and formal gowns ,and she feels different and alienated. Also when she sees Will, she really gets tense and feels awkward, so she can't be sure what she will say or do or how she looks like. Besides this, I think that she can be only excited ,and can't know what to do, because she goes to rich people's wedding ,and they are high society.

**(...)Kayla wasn't able to grasp the fact that Ronnie was happy simply being with Will(...)She knew she'd changed in the weeks she'd been down here(...) Pg.263**

It shows us that Ronnie now wants a permanent and long lasting emotional relationship like Will. Also Ronnie compares relationship in New York with their relationships, and thinks that in New York they always go the clubs, and music is too loud, and everyone only wants to have fun, and is on the make. Moreover she realizes that she has no interest in going to clubs anymore, and thinks that Kayla, who is her best friend, doesn't fathom how Ronnie can be happy with Will, because it isn't a relationship that she used to have in New York, since it contains passion, love , loyalty and understanding.

**"You didn't ruin the wedding," she said with a wry smile. "You made the reception... memorable..." (...)"Partly because I talked to Will. But the main reason I came is because I want to know something. And I want you to tell me the truth." Ronnie felt her stomach roiling. "What do you want to know?" "I want to know if you love my brother." (...)"It's not a summer fling?" Pg. 273**
**"I believe you ."(...) "I've been around. I've seen that look before. Like this morning when I looked in the mirror. I feel the same way about Daniel, but I have to say it's a little odd to see that look on you. When I was seventeen, I don't think I even knew what love was. But when it's right, it's right, and you just know it." (...)She was the kind of person Ronnie**

**wanted to be in a few years, in practically every way. In a matter of minutes, Megan had become her hero. Pg. 274**

Megan says it to Ronnie, after Megan's mother criticizes Ronnie for her materials wealth. It shows us that both Ronnie and Megan fall in love deeply with full of emotion, so Megan understands how Ronnie feels and thinks clearly. Also their love seem to me real and lingering ,and in this part, Megan seems to Ronnie like an understanding, kind , heroic, lovely and helpful girl ,and longs for a friend like her for this summer, because she hasn't got any real girlfriend there ,and has got a lot hassles.

**As soon as she was close, she threw her arms around him and kissed him as passionately as she could.(...) And I need you to do something for me." When he cocked his head questioningly, she went on. "Play today like you've never played before." Pg. 276**

Ronnie says it to Will, when Will is in the volleyball match. From this quote we learn that Ronnie motivates him ,and she seems like a unique inspiration for Will. After their longing and emotional kiss Will's team starts playing remarkably good ,and Will also plays very well ,and scores a lot. Sometimes he looks to Ronnie sitting in the bleachers opposite his parents. At the end their team advances to the semi-finals, and Will tries to find Ronnie for thanking her for her supports.

**The Last Song** **07.03.10**

**Chapter 27:**

Quotes/Passages from this chapter:

**Now, however, he was plagued by the feeling that he'd made a mistake. Perhaps he'd pushed his luck too far in making the Blakelees the target of his latest project. They were the closest thing to royalty in Wilmington, after all—they had power, they had connections, and they had money.(...) The buildings he'd burned and the people he'd hurt meant absolutely nothing to him, but the thought of prison made him... sick. And never once had the fear felt closer than it had since last night. Pg. 278**
**The possibility hit him like a physical blow. Where he'd once had complete power over Will, their roles had suddenly been reversed... or at least equalized. Pg. 279**

I think that Marcus is afraid of being captured ,and sending to the jail, so in the previous chapters , he seems like a fearless boy and doesn't afraid of anything. Also he doesn't feel nervous and scared of the other things he does with the fire. For instance, he harms Blaze with fire ,and then escapes without considering how Blaze is . However I think that the reason why he gets really anxious is that he makes a mistake by annoying rich and prosperous Blakelee family. Also they can call the police, and police will definitely believe them because of their material wealth and respectability.

**The Last Song** **13.03.10**

**Chapter 28:**

My Feelings About The Events:

**He was certain the first thing Marcus would do if arrested would be to get his sentence reduced in exchange for "useful information" about another, more serious crime—Scott's. It would cause problems for Scott at a critical time in his scholarship search, not to mention hurt Scott's parents—who also happened to be close friends of his own parents. So he'd lied, and unfortunately his mom had chosen to blame the whole thing on Ronnie. Pg. 281**

It shows us that Will can't decide clearly, because when he says something about Marcus to the police, Marcus tells to the police Scott's church fire accident, and they arrest him, so Scott can't be accepted to the school that he wants to go. Also when Will doesn't do something to support Ronnie about the wedding disaster, his mother blames Ronnie for all of the wedding events ,and Will rarely can speak with her ,so their relationship gets worse.

**"But everything has changed," Pastor Harris countered. "Because I know?" "No," he said. "Because of the time you've spent together. Before the two of you came down, he was so nervous. Not about being sick, but because of how much he wanted to spend time with you, and wanted everything to go well. I don't think you realize how much he missed you, or how much he really loves you and Jonah. He was literally counting the days. When I'd see him, he'd say, 'Nineteen days,' or, 'Twelve days.' And the day before you arrived? He spent hours cleaning the house and putting new sheets on the beds. I know the place isn't much, but if you'd seen it before, you'd understand. He wanted the two of you to have a summer to remember, and he wanted to be part of that. Like all parents, he wants you to be happy. He wants to know that you're going to be okay. He wants to know that you'll make good decisions. That's what he needed this summer, and that's what you've given him." pg. 319**
**"But I haven't always made good decisions." (...) But I do know how proud he is of the young woman you've become. He told me that just a few days ago, and you should have seen him when he spoke about you. He was so... proud, so happy (...) pg. 320**
**"I was so mean to him. I quit the piano! I blamed him for everything, and I didn't say more than a few words to him for three years! Three years! And I can't get those years back. But maybe if I hadn't been so angry, he might not have gotten sick. Maybe I caused that extra... stress that did all this. Maybe it was me!" pg. 321**
**She didn't want that to happen to her dad. She didn't want him forgotten in a matter of weeks—he was good man, a good father, and he deserved more than that. Pg. 317**
**"I think you're a terrific young lady. I never want you to forget how proud I am of you." Pg. 301**

Ronnie says it to Pastor Harris, when her father is in the hospital. It shows us that she regrets that she doesn't spend much time with his father like a special father-child moment. Also she thinks that she is the main reason of his father's illness, but I feel that she shouldn't be regretful , because she also spends much time together with her father ,and they know each other well. Besides this, her father sees the changes in Ronnie's behaviours especially her change from a rebellious teen to a kind and nice young lady. Similarly Steve makes stained glass with his son Jonah, so he shares a lot of things with his children ,and Ronnie starts thinking to make a meaningful gift for her dad in this chapter ,so when we look at her attitudes in last chapters ,and compare them with these chapters, we can say that she becomes more compassionate instead of mean, more kind instead of rebellious and ungrateful. Also according to all the things that she achieves in her last summer with her father, I think that she and her brother give him the most remarkable and memorable gift in the world, so it is "learning to be a family and share together as a family".

Quotes/Passages from this chapter:

**"Of course I'll wait," he said quietly. "I'll be right here for as long as you need me." Pg. 316**
**"I'll stay tonight so if anything happens and you have to go, someone can be with Jonah. I can stay around here as long as you need me to.(...) pg. 321**

Will says to Ronnie, when her father hospitalizes ,and they wait for him. From this quote we can understand that Will seems like a good friend, because good friends are understanding, sympathetic, and sticks together especially in bad times and good times. Similarly Will understands her situation ,and gives her reasonable advices ,and wants to help her by staying and waiting there when Ronnie goes to the home to look after Jonah. Also he shows that he cares about her father's situation and her family. Besides this, it is really important for a friend to be compassionate. For example, in this part of the novel Will thinks about Jonah as well, because Jonah also needs Ronnie's care.

**Similar Quote:**
**(...)"But you only called twice." "Because I knew your dad needed you," he said, "and I wanted you to concentrate on him, not me. I remember how it was when Mikey died, and I remember wishing that I'd had more time with him. I couldn't do that to you." Pg.383**

**<u>The Last Song 14.03.10</u>**

**Chapter 32:**

SURPRISING PART:

**(...)he reflected that he wanted to be the same kind of father someday. (...)He knew he was lucky, and it was true that things had been a lot better lately. But growing up hadn't been all cupcakes and parties, and he could remember wishing for a different life. But Steve was an altogether different kind of parent. (...)He'd even boarded up the alcove because she didn't want to be reminded of it. What kind of person would do that? Only Steve, a man he'd grown to admire, a man he'd learned from, and the kind of man he himself hoped to be as he grew older. Pg. 324**

In this part of the novel, Will wants to be and have a father like Steve, but when I see it, I am surprised, because his relationship with this father seems good ,and I love the way his father spends his time with Will such as playing airplanes ,so I think that he is a playful and enjoyable man. Besides this, he also provides money for everything that he wants, and Will has got an enormous house, and possibilities. Also his father isn't unconcerned about Will, so he doesn't let him free like snobby rich people's children. For example, Will works in his father's drain company even though they are too rich and he doesn't have to work. Another example of it is he wants to provide best education and job for him, and sends him to a special school that gives a high education.

**"But he's my friend..." (...)"Scott's my friend," he protested. "I can't just... throw him to the wolves." Pg. 331**
**"Go! You're leaving anyway, and we're never going to see each other again. Summers always come to an end. We can talk and pretend all we want, but we can't change that, so let's just end it here and now. I can't handle all this right now, and I can't be with someone I don't trust." Her eyes glittered with unshed tears. "I don't trust you, Will. You need to go." He couldn't move, couldn't speak. "Leave!" she shouted, and ran back to the house. Pg. 332**

It makes me surprised, because they break up because of Scott's fire accident, and I think that it is meaningless, because I suppose that their love will last longer ,and they can't be separated because of a reason like that. Also I believe that Ronnie can't think clearly because of her father's illness ,and she judges Will wrongly ,so Will is right in one point. It is that a trustworthy and good friend must support his/her friend even though he/she can't accept ,and Will does what he should do, but Ronnie gets angry ,because the church is important for her father, so her father always goes there to play piano or pray or speak with Pastor Harris ,and I can say that it is her father's second home where he feels comfortable and relaxed.

Quotes/Passages from this chapter:

**"And now I can't reach the middle part of the window! I'm too short! But I have to finish it, because maybe if I finish it, then Dad will get better. He has to get better, so I tried to use the chair to reach the middle of the window, but it broke and I fell into the glass and I got mad and then I wanted to use the crate, but it's too heavy—" pg. 327 (...)"What about the window? It has to be finished." Pg. 328**

From this quote we see that Jonah is too defiant, and wants to finish the stained glass even though it is too hard for him ,so we can see how he loves his father ,and their sharing is essential for him. After that, Will and Ronnie realizes how Jonah's situation is undesirable and finishing the stained glass is hard and impossible for him to repair, and then they start helping to him ,and together they finish it with a great proud. Besides this, Jonah seems a little naive, because he thinks that when he finishes the stained glass, his dad will be better and might heal quickly even though it is impossible to heal him by repairing their unique stained glass. On the other hand, it means a lot to them although it doesn't make his father better physically, but it can make him feel better mentally, so it is Jonah's precious and unique gift for his father.

**The Last Song** **20.03.10**

**Chapter 34:**

Quotes/Passages from this chapter:

**He didn't clasp his hands or bow his head; he didn't ask to be healed. He did, however, share with God the concerns he had regarding his children. (...) Steve loved his children**

**more than life itself, but more than that, he knew that Jonah needed him, and once more, he was struck by the realization that he was failing as a father. Pg. 343-344**

**"I want you to know that you're the best son a dad could hope to have. I've always been so proud of you, and I know you're going to grow up and do wonderful things. I love you so much." Pg. 344**
**"I'm going to miss you, too. But I'm always going to watch over you, okay? I promise. Do you remember the window we made together?" Jonah nodded, his little jaw quivering. "I call it God Light, because it reminds me of heaven. Every time the light shines through the window we built or any window at all, you'll know I'm right there with you, okay? That's going to be me. I'll be the light in the window." Pg. 345**

Steve seems like a concerned and self-sacrifice father, because at the first he thinks only his children's health, education, life and problems. Also he says that he always watches them ,and it means that he wants them to remember their father in their heart forever even though his body will leave them alone and in agony. I think that it is a good way to remember your relatives especially who died is using your heart to keep them into your most lovely place.

**The Last Song** **20.03.10**

**Chapter 35:**

**According to her father and chapter 35 and epilogue: What does Ronnie learn in this summer with his father?**

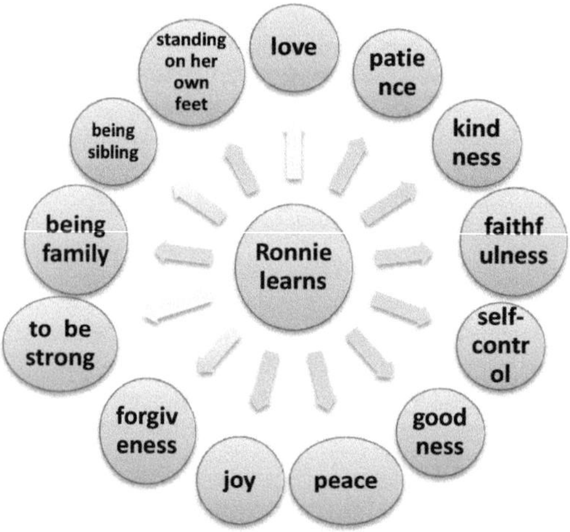


SURPRISING PART:
**In the morning, she woke up eager and anxious to show him what she'd done. But when she entered his bedroom, he wouldn't stir at all, and she panicked when she realized that he was barely breathing. Her stomach was in knots as she called the ambulance, and she felt unsteady as she made her way back to the bedroom. She wasn't ready, she told herself, she hadn't shown him the song. She needed another day. *It's not time yet. Pg. 371***
**When he rolled his head with great effort to look at her, she saw a darkness in his eyes that she'd never seen before. But then he blinked and she heard him sigh. Pg. 372**

It makes me surprised, because when we look at Ronnie's eagerness, we can say that she her day will get good, but then we see that her father starts to get worse, and she must take it to the hospital. However she is too nervous, and doesn't want that this day is the last day of her father.

MY FAVORITE PART:

***In all honesty, you might not, and that would hurt me more than you could ever imagine. You and Jonah have always meant so much to me(...) pg. 350.***

**"You want to do something special. Something that means a lot to him." pg. 351**

**It was a good day, a day she knew she'd always remember. But as she sat alone in the living room after her dad had gone to bed, she once again found herself thinking that there was something more she could do for him. pg. 353**

**She would watch him in silence, chafing at the knowledge that there was something more she could do, if only she knew what it was. Pg. 365**

**It was the song he'd been writing, the song she'd heard him playing that night in the church. She set the pages on top of the table to inspect them more closely. Her eye raced over the heavily edited series of notes, and she thought again that her dad had been on to something.(...) she thought she recognized where the composition began to lose its way. She fished a pencil from the table drawer and began to overlay her own work on his, scrawling rapid chord progressions and melodic riffs where her father had left off. Pg. 370-371 (...) Despite his condition, it seemed to dawn on him what Ronnie had done. Ever so gradually, she saw his grimace replaced by an expression of wonder. As he stared at the piano standing exposed in the alcove, she knew she had done the right thing. Leaning over, she kissed him on the cheek. "I finished your song," she said. "Our last song. And I want to play it for you." Pg.375**

**Instead, she stared out at the freezing December rain and spoke of her last recital, the most important recital of her life. "I played for him as long as I could, Mom. And I tried so hard to make it beautiful for him, because I knew how much it meant to him. But he was just so weak," she whispered. "At the end, I'm not sure he could even hear me." Pg. 377**

Ronnie wants to make something, which means a lot to her father, and she thinks that she can finish his father's last song that he starts it in the church but he can't continue to compose because of his illness, and it is important for her father, because it is the only thing that they share together. Also it is their last song, because his father will die, and Ronnie thinks that she can only remember him by listening and feeling, harmony, memories and notes in his songs such as their last song. After he listens their last song, he thinks that life is a song like their last song. Besides this, what a father can expect from his children ....Also he is proud of Ronnie, because he sees that she changes from an intransigent girl to a compassionate young lady, and plays their songs intensely. After it, Steve finds presence of God, and it is what he shares with his children. Also she gives him the best gift before his death. After this event, she continues to play for him as long as she can ,and tries so hard to make it beautiful for him, because she knows how much it means to him. Besides this, their last score is a symbol for her dad, and when she tucks his beloved score under her arm, she thinks that he will always with her.

**The Last Song** **21.03.10**

**Chapter 36:**

Quotes/Passages from this chapter:

**He finally understood that God's presence was everywhere, at all times, and was experienced by everyone at one time or another. It had been with him in the workshop as he'd labored over the window with Jonah; it had been present in the weeks he'd spent with Ronnie. It was present here and now as his daughter played their song, the last song they would ever share. (...) pg. 375**

From this quote we understand that God's presence for him is spending time together with his family and sharing some unique moments as a family particularly with his son and daughter ,and he doesn't forget it even though he will die. Also I think that he is lucky because God gives them the best gift ever before his death. Everyone wants to share these special moments with their children ,and Steve and his family does it as well. Besides this, they are his last memories ,and Ronnie's song is the last song he will hear expect God's sound that calls him to the heaven.

<u>**The Last Song 21.03.10**</u>

**Epilogue:**

Quotes/Passages from this chapter:

**Staying with and caring for her dad had changed her, and she knew that she would survive. That's what her dad would have wanted, and she could almost hear him reminding her that she was stronger than she realized. He wouldn't want her to mourn for months; he would want her to live her life much the way he had in the final year of his own life. More than anything, he wanted her to embrace life and flourish. Pg. 384**

It shows us that she matures, and tries to find a way to stand on her own feet, and be strong even though the obstacles, and problems. Also it can be an evident of the lesson that she learns during the summer. Besides this, she learns that life goes on anyway, and how to be strong even though life goes bad. Furthermore I think that she learns a lot by spending her time with her father.

**"When are you getting in?"**
**"Let's see..." She could almost see him squinting at his watch. "I landed a little more than an hour ago."**
**"You're here? Where are you?"**
**It took him a moment to respond, and when she heard his voice again, she realized it wasn't coming from the phone. It was coming from behind her. Turning, she saw him in the doorway, holding his phone. Pg. 388**
**"Well, the school doesn't normally allow midyear transfers, but my mom's on the board of trustees at Vanderbilt and she happened to know some people at this other university and was able to pull some strings. Anyway, I found out while I was in Europe that I'd been accepted, so I'm going to transfer. I start there next semester and thought you might want to know."(...) "Where are you going to go?" "Columbia."For an instant, she wasn't sure**

**she'd heard him right. "You mean Columbia as in New York Columbia?" (...)Will was going to go to school here. In New York. With her. (...)knowing that nothing could ever be better than this moment, right now. Pg. 389-390**
**When he met her eyes, she saw the young man she'd loved last summer and the young man she still loved now. "I never stopped loving you, Ronnie. And I never stopped thinking about you. Even if summers do come to an end." She smiled, knowing he was telling the truth.**
**"I love you, too, Will Blakelee," Pg. 390**

Their love will be permanent and passionate, because they don't separate, so I think that when they have got a long distance between them, they might have got problems ,and break up, but they are close ,and the author makes a happy ending that we don't expect ,and isn't predictable. However I love the end, because I think that they must be together, so they fit together perfectly.

LETTER TO THE AUTHOR:

**27.03.10**

Dear Nicholas Sparks,

First of all I must thank you for writing this unique, glorious, wonderful and lovely book named "The Last Song". I think the way you create the characters and give them some behaviours is brilliant especially the way you make Ronnie from a stubborn girl to a mature young lady makes the book more remarkable. Also I should say that the love between Ronnie and Will is absolutely splendid and impressive like they are real. Their love, problems, obstacles such as Will's mother Susan, Ronnie's struggle against the summer place, Marcus, Ashley and the important moments in our lives such as being a family, being in love passionately and permanently, and sharing moments with our friends and families are worked up marvellously in this novel. You really impacts on our lives, because this novel can teach us that there are significant moments that we mustn't miss them and regret what we miss. For example, Ronnie regrets that she should spend more time together with her father before he died. Also the love between parents and children (Ronnie-Steve) brothers and sisters (Ronnie-Jonah, Megan-Will) and a young love (Will- Ronnie) develop really animatedly. Besides them, it's not only about love, so it is about family, fate and forgiveness.

There are many characters in the novel, and they have got many different qualities. Then we see their developments. However, Jonah is my favourite character in this book, because he is amazingly funny, sarcastic, enthusiastic and playful. I love the way he tricks his sister, and reacts to their situations and to Ronnie. Also he is too optimistic, so he finds his father's old and ruined house funny and awesome. My second favourite character is Ronnie, but at the beginning she seems like a stubborn, grouchy and bad tempered girl, and I don't like her decisions, behaviours and relationship with her dad, brother, and Blaze. At the beginning she joins to a bad crowd which includes the antagonist Marcus ,but she changes gradually after she falls in love with Will, so she becomes a lovely, live, kind, grateful and honest girl instead of a girl who does the opposite of what her parents say to her or what she must do.

Another point is the points of view of all the characters switch chapter by chapter, and I really find it important for reader to understand all of the feelings and thoughts of the characters and the reader has got a chance to see into the thoughts of all the characters.

In this novel there are things about presence of God, praying and hope, so it is developed by Pastor Harris who is a very intimate friend of Steve and his piano teacher. Pastor Harris used to talk with him about God's presence, Steve's questions and hearing God. However the part (Galatians 5:22) of the Bible in this novel "But when the Holy Spirit controls our lives, he will produce this kind of fruit in us: love, joy, peace, patience, kindness, goodness, faithfulness, gentleness, and self-control." explains the changes in Ronnie the best and fits with Ronnie's situation. Besides this I have started your novel "A Walk To Remember". Similarly at the beginning of this novel, there are things related to religions , but in next chapters there are many ,and I should say that in The Last Song there aren't as religious subject as A Walk To Remember ,and it makes the novel more understandable for me, because I don't know every words related to religious subject ,and I get bored when I look up every single word. Then I lose my concentration ,and don't understand anything, so I reread it again. For me, religion is important but in your book and religious words make reader bored ,and put the book away sometimes. Also you can try to minimize them.

Besides this religious subjects, after the church fire and the broken stained glass, Steve wants to make a new stained glass, and during the summer he works with Jonah, so it is the best thing they share together before he died. Similarly I find the last part of the novel incredibly superb, because in the last part Ronnie completes the last song of her father before he died. Then he plays it to him, and I think that what a father can want any more from his son / daughter. Then Jonah wants to finish the stained glass before his father will die, but he can't do it individually, so Ronnie and Will want to help him intensely. Firstly, Jonah teaches them how Ronnie and Will can repair and put the little parts in it. Then they work together ,and the unique stained glass is finished.

My favourite dramatic part of this novel is when Ronnie wants to stay with her dad even though he will die, and she wants to make something special for her father like finishing his last song. However I feel upset, when she finishes their last song, and wants to show it to her dad eagerly, because when she finds her dad, he doesn't stir at all and barely breathes. On the other hand, there are moments that make me feel full of love and hope. For instance, when Will says that he will stay in New York, I feel the happiness deeply, and feel glad that they can see each other ,and their relationship will stay permanently and passionately, so their love will not be a summer love.

As my final words, I really love the atmosphere, characters, places, conflicts, developments of characters , the classic music, piano , love between the characters, the moments in the lives, the changes ,the last memories and sharing things with someone in this novel. I really appreciate you because of your great work, novel and coming movie. Also I want to watch your The Last Song movie. Thank you for presenting a kind of novel like this.

*Sincerely Boğaç Aybey*

## VOCABULARY JOURNAL

| Word | Form of the word | Meaning of the word | Example Sentence | Synonym |
|---|---|---|---|---|
| | | **Prologue** | | |
| **Pastor** | noun | A Christian priest in some Protestant churches. | The pastor in the church gave a sermon to the local people. | Priest |
| **Arson** | noun | The crime of deliberately making something burn, especially a building. | When the building burnt, the police suspected of arson. | Vandalism |
| **Hindsight** | noun | The ability to understand a situation only after it has happened. | With hindsight, she suspected of him, but she wasn't sure. | Retrospect |
| | | **Chapter 1** | | |
| **Godforsaken** | adjective | A godforsaken place is far away from where people live and contains nothing interesting, attractive, or cheerful. | Why do we go every summer to this godforsaken summer house in this remote town? | Abandoned, deserted, remote, isolated |
| **Armpit of something** | noun | The ugliest or worst place in a particular city or area. | He thinks that his neighbourhood is the armpit of Manhattan, because it is too dirty, and in the night it isn't safe because of the drug sellers, and gangs. | Sunken or decayed area |
| **Curfew** | noun | The time, decided by a parent, by which a child must be home or asleep in the evening. | She must be in home at 10 o'clock, because of her curfew. | Late hour check in time, time limit |
| | | **Chapter 2** | | |
| **Keyed-up** | adjective | Worried or excited. | Before his first job, he was keyed-up, but gradually he adjusts to his firm. | Agitated |
| **Presence of** | noun | When someone or something is present in a particular place. | Some people don't experience the presence of God, so they don't believe God. | Being |
| **All-American** | adjective | Having qualities that are considered to be typically American and that American people admire, such as being healthy and working hard. | Firstly, she seems an all-American girl which is healthy, and works hard. | Typical American |

| | | | | |
|---|---|---|---|---|
| | | **Chapter 3** | | |
| **Distracted** | adjective | Anxious and unable to think clearly. | In the morning, he is too distracted that he can't think clearly. | Anxious, troubled |
| **Gasket** | noun | **Blow a gasket -** To become very angry. | My mother blows a gasket, when I come late home in the evening. | Angry |
| **To drench** | verb | To make something or someone extremely wet. | When he doesn't wake up easily in the mornings, his mother drenches him. | Splash, wet |
| | | **Chapter 4** | | |
| **To ditch** | verb | To leave someone you are within a place without telling them you are going. | Some teenagers ditch their parents, because they have got family problems. | Run away |
| **Case** | noun | **Case in point** - A clear example of something that you are discussing or explaining. | Jack's career is a case in point, so we are discussing it now, because his career is getting worse. | Example |
| **Antsy** | adjective | Nervous and unable to keep still because you are waiting for something to happen. | She was antsy in the hospital last night, because her mother was in intensive care, so she waited for her mother. | Nervous, restless |
| | | **Chapter 5** | | |
| **Self-possessed** | adjective | Calm, confident, and in control of your feelings, even in difficult or unexpected situations – used to show approval. | He was too self-possessed, even though his mother was in the intensive care. | Confident, assertive, sure of yourself |
| **Exhale** | verb | To breathe air, smoke etc out of your mouth. | The runner exhaled, because he was too nervous, and wanted to be relaxing. Then started to the race. | Breath out, blow |
| **Hyped up** | adjective | Very excited or nervous, and unable to keep still. | He was hyped up, because he waited his father in the hospital, so he couldn't keep his nerves, and feelings. | Overexcited |
| | | **Chapter 6** | | |
| **Overprotective** | adjective | So anxious to protect someone from harm that you restrict their freedom. | Her parents are too overprotective, so they are worried about her, and restrict her | Protective, wrap somebody in cotton wool, |

| | | | | |
|---|---|---|---|---|
| | | | freedom. Consequently she gets bored. | anxious |
| **Stunt** | noun | Something that is done to attract people's attention, especially in advertising or politics. | These slogans aren't too attractive, and many politicians say that it is only a little, and miserable stunt for their party. | Attention |
| **To swivel** | verb | To turn around quickly and face a different direction, or to make something do this. | He swivelled around to look at the raging fire at the church. | Turn, twist, spin |
| | | **Chapter 7** | | |
| **To harangue** | verb | To speak in a loud angry way, often for a long time, in order to criticize someone or to persuade them that you are right. | He always harangues us with his angry and loud voice, so we can't say anything to him. | Declaim, accost |
| **Dubious** | adjectiv e | Probably not honest, true, right etc. | The new plan is dubious, because we can think that it isn't true. | Suspicious |
| **To pique** | verb | **Pique your interest/curiosity:** To make you feel interested in something or someone. | The new girl in the class piqued my curiosity. | Motivate, being curiosity |
| | | **Chapter 8** | | |
| **To nauseate** | verb | To make someone feel that they are going to vomit. | Some alcohols nauseated him, so he never wants to drink them anymore. | Vomit |
| **To shoplift** | verb | To take something from a shop without paying for it. | I saw a woman wants to take those CDs without paying, so I called the police, after she shoplifted. | Steal |
| **Get-together** | noun | A friendly informal meeting or party. | They invited us to the get-together. | Party |
| | | **Chapter 9** | | |
| **Sturdy** | adjectiv e | Determined and not easily persuaded to change your opinions. | We can't convince him easily, so he is a sturdy person. | Determined, scornful |
| **Encounte r** | noun | An occasion when you meet or experience something. | A child's first encounter with books is too important. | Meeting |
| **Grimace** | noun | An expression you make by twisting your face because you do not like something or because you are feeling pain. | When he comes to the room, we can easily see the grimace of pain in his face. | Frown, smirk |
| | | **Chapter 10** | | |

| | | | | |
|---|---|---|---|---|
| **Earnest** | adjectiv e | Very serious and sincere. | I don't like him, when his face is too earnest. | Serious, severe, honest |
| **Throwba ck** | noun | Something that is similar to something that existed in the past, or belongs to the past. | Her dresses are throwback to the 1900s. | Similar |
| **Denial** | noun | A condition in which you refuse to admit or believe that something bad exists or has happened in denial. | He is in denial, and refuses to believe that he has got a severe illness. | Dismissal, refusal of belief in |
| | | **Chapter 11** | | |
| **Stoic** | adjectiv e | Someone who does not show their emotions and does not complain when bad things happen to them. | She is a stoic and quite girl, so she doesn't show her emotions, and often complains when bad things happen. | Philosophic, calm |
| **To clench** | verb | **Clench your fists/teeth/jaw etc:** To hold your hands, teeth etc together tightly, usually because you feel angry or determined. | He wants to run 10 km., and he clenches his teeth. Then he starts running with a great determinant. | Grasp |
| **Mortified** | adjectiv e | Extremely offended, ashamed, or embarrassed. | When his friends ridiculed with him, he felt mortified. | Sheepish, awkward, humiliated |
| | | **Chapter 12** | | |
| **Groundin g** | noun | A punishment for a child's bad behaviour in which they are not allowed to go out with their friends for a period of time. | When she doesn't obey her mother, her mother notices her grounding. | Punishment |
| **To stifle** | verb | To stop a feeling from being expressed. | He can't stifle his smile. | Hide, suppress |
| **Felony** | adjectiv e | A serious crime such as murder. | She doesn't want to commit a felony shoplifting anymore. | Misdemeanou r |
| | | **Chapter 13** | | |
| **Cold shoulder** | noun | (give somebody/get) The cold shoulder to behave in an unfriendly way towards someone that you know. | He always gives his friends cold shoulder, so he is too unfriendly and rude. | Rude, unfriendly, hostile, cold, antagonistic |
| **Cynical** | adjectiv e | Unwilling to believe that people have good, honest, or sincere reasons for doing something. | Since her boyfriend tricked her, she became very cynical about men. | Disbelief, sceptical |
| **Unfazed** | adjectiv e | Not confused or shocked by a difficult situation or by something bad that has happened. | We can't believe how he can be so unfazed, and isn't shocked by his brothers' death. | Calm, stay cool, keep cool |
| | | **Chapter 14** | | |

| | | | | |
|---|---|---|---|---|
| **Acquiescent** | adjective | Too ready to agree with someone or do what they want, without complaining or saying what you want to do. | His behaviours become more acquiescent, but later he was too determined and stubborn. | Passive, |
| **Inward** | adjective | Felt or experienced in your own mind but not expressed to other people. | He felt an inward panic inside, but he can't express it to the other people. | Inside, inwards |
| **To convey** | verb | To communicate or express something, with or without using words. | He conveyed his feeling to the audience. | Express, communicate |
| | | **Chapter 15** | | |
| **Urge** | noun | A strong wish or need. | I have a strong urge to be with her. | Desire |
| **To force** | verb | **Force a smile/laugh etc:** To make yourself smile, laugh etc even though you feel upset or annoyed. | She always wants to smile even though she feels upset, so sometimes we think that she forces a smile. | Make somebody to do |
| **Kicker** | noun | A surprising or important ending to something. | The kicker comes at the end of the story, when the character. | Ironic ending |
| | | **Chapter 16** | | |
| **Rapport** | noun | Friendly agreement and understanding between people. | He always wants their rapport with their friends alive and continuous. | Relationship |
| **Serene** | adjective | Very calm or peaceful. | I can't understand how a person can so serene in her situation. | Calm, undisturbed |
| **Inevitable** | adjective | Certain to happen and impossible to avoid. | It's inevitable that he will find the reality as soon as possible. | Certain, definite |
| | | **Chapter 17** | | |
| **Exasperation** | noun | When you feel annoyed because someone continues to do something that is upsetting you. | His continuous exasperation makes me feel upset. | Anger, annoyance |
| **Inscrutable** | adjective | Someone who is inscrutable shows no emotion or reaction in the expression on their face so that it is impossible to know what they are feeling or thinking. | She looked for some answers, but her expression remained inscrutable. | Expressionless, blank |
| **Doormat** | noun | Someone who lets other people treat them badly and never complains. | Don't let him treat you like a doormat! | Be under somebody's control |
| | | **Chapter 18** | | |

| | | | | |
|---|---|---|---|---|
| **Constern ation** | noun | A feeling of worry, shock, or fear. | To my consternation, I found the taxi was empty. | Alarm |
| **Enigmatic** | adjectiv e | Mysterious and difficult to understand. | She gave me an enigmatic smile, so I can't understand its meaning easily. | Mysterious |
| **Intuit** | verb | To know or guess something because of a feeling you have, rather than because of facts you know. | She seemed to intuit that he didn't want to say anything more. | Perceive |

## CONTEXT OF CLUES:

**Prologue:**

**Fascinated (adjective):** *At this year, they had the beach pretty much to themselves, but Jonah showed* ***no interest*** *in either the waves or the seagulls that had* ***fascinated*** *him only a few months earlier.* **(Antonym)**

**Chapter 1:**

**Banishment (noun):** *That was* ***banishment****, and for most of the nine hours it had taken them to drive down,* ***she'd felt like a prisoner being transferred to a rural penitentiary****.* **(Description)**

**Chapter 2:**

**Gregarious (adjective):** *Unlike Kim, who'd been* ***outgoing*** *and* ***gregarious****, he'd always been more reticent and blended into crowds.* **( Synonym )**

**Chapter 3:**

**Packed (adjective):** *The place was* ***packed. Old and young, families, groups of middle-schoolers*** *ogling one another.* **(Example)**

**Chapter 4:**

**Flaunt (verb):** *Because he didn't like* ***people with money,*** *didn't like the way they* ***flaunted*** *it, and didn't like the way they thought they were* ***better than other people*** *because of* ***it****.* **(Combination of clues)**

**Chapter 5:**

**Rusty (adjective) :***"I **haven't taken a shot since the season ended**, and I wanted to see how **rusty** I am."* **( Cause and effect)**

**Chapter 6:**

**Haul away (verb):** *The rides had been **disassembled** and the booths had already been **hauled away, leaving behind only scattered** garbage and food remnants.* **(Combination of clues)**

**Chapter 7:**

**Shallow (adjective):** *In Ashley's world, everyone and everything was put into neat **little** boxes: **popular or not, expensive or cheap, rich or poor, beautiful or ugly**. And he'd eventually grown tired of her **shallow** value judgments and her inability to accept or appreciate anything in between.* **( Series )**

**Chapter 8:**

**Resemblance (noun) :** *"They're **brothers**," Blaze explained. Ronnie studied them, not seeing the **resemblance**. "You are?"* **(Contrast)**

**Chapter 9:**

**Expressive (adjective) :** *(...)she told the counsellor that Steve **kept his feelings bottled up inside** but that it wasn't his fault. Neither of his parents had been **expressive** people (...)* **(Contrast)**

**Chapter 10:**

**Vinyl (noun):** *In addition to CDs, there were actual **vinyl record albums*** (...) **(Example)**

**Chapter 11:**

**Passable (adjective):** *By the end of her life, she'd learned **passable** English, enough to **navigate the bank and grocery store, but even then her accent was heavy enough that it was sometimes difficult for others to understand her.*** **( Comparison and contrast)**

**Chapter 12:**

**Stiff (adjective) :***Her back was stiff, her neck **ached**, and **when she got the courage to sit up, a stabbing pain coursed through her shoulder.*** **( Example)**

**Chapter 13:**

**Baffled (adjective) :** *If he wasn't **confused** before, he was completely **baffled** now.* **(Synonym)**

**Chapter 14:**

**Indication (noun):** *If he heard the door close, he gave no **indication**; **instead, he seemed content to toss tiny seashells at the spider crabs that were scurrying to their holes.*** **(Contrast)**

**Chapter 15:**

**Cool off (verb):** *Marcus turned toward her, feeling the sudden urge to **clear his mind**, to **cool off**.* **(Synonym)**

**Chapter 16:**

**Adrift (adjective) :** *He knew it was a ridiculous fantasy, but without music he felt **aimless** and **adrift**.* **( Synonym )**

**Chapter 17:**

**Wishy washy (adjective) :***There was something so **wishy-washy** and **clueless** about that.* **(Synonym)**

**Chapter 18:**

**Scrimmage (noun):** *They'd finished up at the garage at three and had raced over to the beach for a **scrimmage against a couple of teams from Georgia that were spending the week in the area.*** **( Description )**

## VOCABULARY JOURNAL -2

| Word | Form of the word | Meaning of the word | Example Sentence | Synonym |
|---|---|---|---|---|
| | | **Chapter 19** | | |
| **Oblivious** | Adj. | Not knowing about or not noticing something that is happening around you. | They soon fell asleep, oblivious of the danger. | Unaware |
| **Jocular** | Adj. | Joking or humorous. | I love the way he speak with his jocular tone. | Jolly, humorous |
| **Acutely** | Adv. | Feeling or noticing something very strongly. | I am acutely aware of his girlish voice. | Sharply |
| | | **Chapter 20** | | |
| **Ceaseless** | Adj. | Happening for a long time without stopping. | The boatman fought against the ceaseless wind. | Never-ending |
| **Haul** | Noun | Long/slow haul: Something that takes a lot of time and effort. | They won the match with over a long haul. | Effort |
| **Temptati on** | Noun | A strong desire to have or do something even though you know you should not. | There is always a temptation to blame others for your own problems. | Attraction |
| | | **Chapter 21** | | |
| **Light-hearted** | Adj. | Cheerful and not worried about anything. | Jonah seems like a light-hearted boy, because he only wants to have fun, and be cheerful. | Amusing |
| **Nonchala nt** | Adj. | Behaving calmly and not seeming interested in anything or worried about anything. | I don't understand how she is still nonchalant even though her son wasn't found. | Unconcerned |
| **Bidding** | Noun | Do sb's bidding : To obey someone's requests or orders. | If he commanded then people wanted to do his bidding. | Obey |
| | | **Chapter 22** | | |
| **To screw** | Verb | An offensive expression used to show that you are very angry with someone. | He wants to forget her, because he screws her. | To be angry |
| **Tease** | Noun | Something that you say or do as a joke, to tease someone. | I'm sorry, it was only a tease. | Joke |
| **Frigid** | Adj. | Not friendly or kind. | I don't like her frigid attitudes. | Cold, icy |
| | | **Chapter 23** | | |
| **To resent** | Verb | To feel angry or upset about a situation or about something that someone has done, especially because you think that it is not fair. | No one resents Ashley's success. | Be in a huff |
| **Idyllic** | Adj. | An idyllic place or time is very | It was an idyllic life for | Blissful |

| | | | | |
|---|---|---|---|---|
| | | beautiful, happy, and peaceful, with no problems or dangers. | both of them, and they hated to leave the country. | |
| **Needy** | Adj. | Needing and wanting a lot of love and attention. | The children ,who live on the streets, are needy. | In need, poor |
| | | **Chapter 24** | | |
| **Gross** | Adj. | Very unpleasant to look at or think about. | It is too gross to think about their nasty kiss. | Nasty |
| **Distractio n** | Noun | Something that stops you paying attention to what you are doing. | Other people's talk was just a distraction. | Agitation |
| **Unabate d** | Adj. | Continuing without becoming any weaker or less violent. | I think that his illness is unabated. | Continuous, neverending |
| | | **Chapter 25** | | |
| **Crutch** | Noun | Something that gives someone support or help, especially something that is not really good for them. | As things got worse at work, he began to use alcohol as a crutch. | Aid |
| **Content ment** | Noun | The state of being happy and satisfied. | The people of the village seem to live in peace and contentment. | Happiness |
| **Balmy** | Adj. | balmy air, weather etc is warm and pleasant | It was a balmy night with a full moon. | Mild |
| | | **Chapter 26** | | |
| **Conscien ce** | Noun | The part of your mind that tells you whether what you are doing is morally right or wrong. | I have to do what my conscience tells me. | Guilt |
| **Conceiva ble** | Adj. | Able to be believed or imagined. | It is conceivable that we could solve all our problems. | Possibly |
| **To extricate** | Verb | To escape from a difficult or embarrassing situation, or to help someone escape. | He wants to extricate himself from this embarrassing situation. | Get away |
| | | **Chapter 27** | | |
| **Nagging** | Adj. | Making you worry or feel pain slightly all the time. | I have a nagging feeling that I forgot to do something. | Perpetual |
| **Glum** | Adj. | If someone is glum, they feel unhappy and do not talk a lot. | Indeed, he had seemed quite glum. | Gloomy |
| **Short-lived** | Adj. | Existing or happening for only a short time. | We were glad to be home, but our happiness was short-lived. | Brief |
| | | **Chapter 28** | | |
| **Unassaila ble** | Adj. | Not able to be criticized, made weaker, or beaten. | It is an unassailable tradition for them. | Certain |
| **Nonethel ess** | Adv. | In spite of the fact that has just been mentioned. | The flowers are beautiful. Nonetheless many people tread | But |

| | | | | |
|---|---|---|---|---|
| | | | them. | |
| **With your tail between your legs** | Noun | Embarrassed or unhappy because you have failed or been defeated. | They walked off the court with their tails between their legs. | Embarrassed |
| | | **Chapter 29** | | |
| **To condone** | Verb | To accept or forgive behaviour that most people think is morally wrong. | Most people don't condone her cruel behaviours. | Believe |
| **To dismantle** | Verb | To gradually get rid of a system or organization. | The society doesn't dismantle the new tax system. | Take apart |
| **Breezy** | Adj. | A breezy person is happy, confident, and relaxed. | She's a woman with a lot of breezy manners. | Relaxed, happy, confident |
| | | **Chapter 30** | | |
| **To incorporate** | Verb | To include something as part of a group, system, plan etc. | Our report software isn't incorporated in the local fair of PC software. | Include |
| **To muse** | Verb | To say something in a way that shows you are thinking about it carefully. | "I remember his name ...." he mused. | Be lost in thought |
| **To fray** | Verb | If someone's temper or nerves fray, or if something frays them, they become annoyed. | Mikey felt his temper begin to fray. | Aggravate |
| | | **Chapter 31** | | |
| **Plea** | Noun | A request that is urgent or full of emotion. | I don't want to hear anyone's plea. | Request |
| **Core** | Noun | To the core: Extremely or completely. | When I heard the news, I was shocked to the core. | Extremely |
| **To portend** | Verb | To be a sign that something is going to happen, especially something bad. | Unfamiliar accidents that portend disaster make me feel worried. | To be the sign |
| | | **Chapter 32** | | |
| **Indication** | Noun | A sign, remark, event etc that shows what is happening, what someone is thinking or feeling, or what is true. | There was no indication of forced entry to the building. | Sign |
| **Harsh** | Adj. | Severe, cruel, or unkind. | I find his behaviours harsh. | Cruel |
| **To quaver** | Verb | If your voice quavers, it shakes as you speak, especially because you are nervous or upset. | Her voice starts quavering, when she says that she loses her son. | Shake |
| | | **Chapter 33** | | |
| **To deflect** | Verb | To take someone's attention away from something. | I don't want him to deflect me working. | Interrupt |
| **Composu** | Noun | The state of feeling or seeming calm. | She was trying to get | Calm |

| | | | | |
|---|---|---|---|---|
| **re** | | | her composure back. | |
| **To suffocate** | Verb | To die or make someone die by preventing them from breathing. | They pushed a plastic bag over his head and almost suffocated him. | Choke |
| | | **Chapter 34** | | |
| **Emaciated** | Adj. | Extremely thin from lack of food or illness. | He was emaciated and half his weight. | Underweight |
| **Inconsolably** | Adj. | So sad that it is impossible for anyone to comfort you. | After the death of her baby she was inconsolable. | Heartbroken |
| **Choke** | Verb | To be unable to breathe properly because something is in your throat or there is not enough air. | He can't breathe easily, so he sometimes chokes. | Suffocate |
| | | **Chapter 35** | | |
| **Arduous** | Adj. | Involving a lot of strength and effort. | We organize an arduous trip to the mountains. | Strenuous |
| **Rueful** | Adj. | Feeling or showing that you wish you had not done something. | Jane looked at her with a rueful smile. | Regretful |
| **To stretch out** | Verb | To lie down, usually in order to sleep or rest. | I'm just going to stretch out on the couch for ten minutes. | Lie down |
| | | **Chapter 36 :It is only 1 page, and there isn't any new vocabulary.** | | |
| | | **Chapter 37** | | |
| **To brim** | Verb | If your eyes brim with tears, or if tears brim from your eyes, you start to cry. | Her eyes brimmed with tears. | Cry, full of tears |
| **Awe** | Noun | A feeling of great respect and liking for someone or something. | He gazed me in awe. | Respect |
| **To besiege** | Verb | If people, worries, thoughts etc besiege you, you are surrounded by them. | She was besieged by a storm of conflicting emotions such as desire ,regret and fear. | Surround |
| | | **Epilogue** | | |
| **Upheaval** | Noun | A very big change that often causes problems. | There are many political upheavals in our city. | Change |
| **To reminisce** | Verb | To talk or think about pleasant events in your past. | We like to reminisce, remembering old times. | Memorize |
| **To alter** | Verb | To change, or to make someone or something change. | I haven't seen him for 9 years ,and when I saw him, I realized that his face altered. | Change |

## CONTEXT OF CLUES -2 :

**Chapter 19 : Cringe ( verb ) :***Will **cringed**. "Dad..."(...) "Don't be **<u>embarrassed</u>**."* ( Description )

**Chapter 20: Infectious (adj.) :***He had this real* ***infectious*** *laugh, and* ***you couldn't help but laugh along with him*** *when something funny happened.* ( Description )

**Chapter 21: Stumble (verb ):** *"I'm glad I was able to keep you from* ***stumbling,"*** *Marcus said. "It wouldn't look good to be all* ***bruised*** *(...)* ( Cause and effect )

**Chapter 22: Devour ( verb ) :** *Fires, especially big ones, moved and danced and* ***destroyed*** *and* ***devoured.*** ( Synonmy )

**Chapter 23: Pointless (adj.) :*****She was locked into her prejudices,*** *so* ***any attempt to change her opinion*** *of Ronnie would be* ***pointless.*** ( Combination of clues )

**Chapter 24: Kiln ( noun ) :** *"But* ***it gets hot.*** *Especially when he runs the* ***kiln.*** *It's like an* ***oven.****"* ( Combination of clues )

**Chapter 25: Approximate ( verb ) :** *(...) he'd tried to* ***approximate*** *something by Schumann; for a few days after that,* ***he'd been inspired more by Grieg.*** ( Example )

**Chapter 26: Tuxedo ( noun ) :***But this was a* ***formal, black-tie wedding****:* ***Tuxedos*** *and* ***gowns*** *were required for guests, not just the wedding party.* ( Combination of clues )

**Chapter 27: Wreaked:** *(...) he should be enjoying the* ***havoc*** *he'd* ***wreaked*** *the previous evening.* ( Description )

**Chapter 28: Spurt ( verb ) :***(...) hands to his face and* ***blood spurting*** *between his fingers,* ***his screams partially muffled by the sound of him gagging.*** ( Description )/ (Cause and effect )

**Chapter 29: Vandal ( noun ):***Pastor Harris is worried some* ***vandals might throw rocks at it.*** ( Description )

**Chapter 30: Metastasize( verb ) :** *He knew what it meant when cancer* ***metastasized,*** *he knew what it meant to* ***have cancer not only in his stomach, but also in his pancreas.*** ( Description )

**Chapter 31: Harbour/Harbor** *(...) he'd* ***harbored*** *his* ***secret.*** ( Description )

**Chapter 32: Solder( verb ) :** *Jonah showed Will how to cut the* ***lead strips*** *and taught Ronnie how to* ***solder;*** *Jonah cut the glass, as he'd been doing most of the summer, and slid them* ***into the lead strips before making room for Ronnie to set the pieces in place.*** (Combination of clues )

**Chapter 33: Outnumbered (adj.) :** *(...) she could hear* ***the panic rising in his voi****ce as he realized he was* ***outnumbered.*** ( Cause and effect )

**Chapter 34: Shudder ( verb ) :** *His* ***birdlike shoulders*** *were* ***shuddering,*** *(...)* ( Combination of clues )

**Chapter 35: Glassy (adj.):** *There were times when his eyes were **glassy** and **<u>out of focus</u>**,* (...) ( Synonym )

**Chapter 36: It is only 1 page, and there isn't any new vocabulary.**

**Chapter 37: Ecstatic (adj.) :** *She didn't know what it meant, that he was here, and wasn't sure whether to feel **ecstatic** or **<u>heartbroken</u>** or both.* ( Contrast )

**Epilogue: Cavernous (adj.):** *There seemed to be a **cavernous** echo behind him, **<u>reminiscent of an airport.</u>*** ( Example )